AREND THEODOOR VAN LEEUWEN

Prophecy in a Technocratic Era

With Foreword by

HARVEY G. COX

Charles Scribner's Sons · NEW YORK

A-2.68[C]

Printed in the United States of America
Library of Congress Catalog Card Number 68-12509

▣ Contents

Christians in the Technical and Social Revolutions of Our Time*

"INCREDIBLY rapid technological change is one of the main characteristics of society today. A new kind of world is being created by it, one that presents man with unprecedented power and freedom while confronting him at the same time with equally unprecedented problems. He will soon be on the moon. He moves himself and his goods to the farthest corner of the earth in hours and before long he will do it in minutes. He creates new parts for worn-out human bodies, regulates his own fertility, communicates by satellite, and synthesizes nourishing food. He solves problems in moments that formerly took centuries, or could not be done at all, and he can regulate biologically, whenever he is ready to do so, whole nations by means of contraceptive hormones. He can also destroy the whole world as he knows it. His knowledge, his skills, and his tools to transform his environment have never been so readily available or so profoundly effective and are becoming more so all the time; it is a technological phenomenon radically new in history which is changing the social order as drastically as did the Industrial Revolution.

* By J. Brooke Mosley (Forward Movement Publications, 1966). The above excerpt is quoted with permission of the publishers.

"Surely, the Christian will see this revolution first of all as a gift of God for the liberation of mankind; he will welcome it and not resist it, encourage it and participate in it with thanks to a living Creator who brought him to this place. But at the same time, he is obliged to be aware of the severe human dislocations and sufferings of those who are the victims of rapid change and the dehumanization that often accompanies it. These effects may seem at first glance to be too subtle for serious Christian concern. An African at Geneva, for instance, impatiently took to task those who were anxiously trying to deal with them: 'For you Westerners to speak of the *problems* of technology is like speaking to me of the problems of overeating when I haven't got any food—the effects of technology may be dehumanizing, as you say, but no more so than poverty!' And in earnest discussion with his sub-section partners, an Asian exclaims, 'You talk about the bad effects of technology, but to me it means water, light, and freedom.' And yet, as Section IV [1] put it, 'Technology is humanizing when it frees man from magic, from material servitude and want, from endemic diseases and hunger, and when it frees man for the new possibilities in leisure, for satisfaction and fulfillment of self, and for new forms of creativity. But technology is dehumanizing when it locks men into meaningless routine, into boredom and loneliness for the individual, into a highly fragmented and fiercely competitive society. . . . Whether the efforts of technology will be good or bad depends on the goals that are presupposed.' "

[1] "Section IV" refers to one of the preparatory volumes issued by the Working Committee on Church and Society prior to the Geneva Conference of 1966 sponsored by the World Council of Churches. The theme of Section IV was "Man and Communities in Changing Societies."

Foreword

by HARVEY G. COX

During every stage of his long development on earth man has had to cope in one way or another with the mystery of the future. Sometimes he did it by examining the entrails of birds. Sometimes he thought he saw the future foretold by the motions of the stars. At other times he consulted gifted seers such as those at the famous Oracle of Delphi. The future is always at best uncertain, and before embarking on a military campaign, a business deal, or a romantic escapade, men have always wished they could have at least some tiny indication beforehand of how it would turn out.

But the whole idea that the future can be seen or predicted is based on a notion of history which runs squarely against the grain of Biblical faith. For the Bible, man is placed in an open field of freedom and accountability by a God who has an *intention* for the world but whose intention must run the radical risk of modification or rejection by a freely choosing man. In the Bible God promises man a future and man hopes for a new world of peace and justice. But man's immaturity and sloth, his fear and his hatred constantly frustrate both God's promise and man's hope. Thus the future is always radically open to man's creativity and imagination but also to his perversity and pride. The history of man from Creation to Last Day is not a drama which has already been written. It is an open-ended scenario which is being composed and acted out from day to day.

Prophecy in the Biblical sense of the word has nothing to do with predicting the future. Rather prophecy is a form of address which calls man to an awareness of his historical responsibility and challenges him to act in freedom, to make choices, rather than to "let nature take its course." True, the prophets of the Old Testament sometimes used the rhetorical device of visions of the future. But they used them to try to rouse the people of Israel out of slumber and into the wakefulness and responsibility required by God. The prophets foretold doom, but only if the people refused to change their ways. If they repented, if they remembered the promises they had exchanged with God, then the doom might be avoided. History was not a predetermined fate. It was radically open to man's exercise of his moral will and human capacity for choice.

Arend van Leeuwen believes that what our technologically defined world needs today is a rebirth of prophecy. We need to move away from the notion that the machine has us in its grip and that we can do little about it, a notion advanced by such people as Jacques Ellul. But technology, van Leeuwen contends, does raise enormously the stakes of the game we are playing. It makes the world a more promising and at the same time a more dangerous place. Every possible new technique should force us, for example, to decide whether we really want to make it or not. Every new technology makes us ask whether we want to use it and if so how and to what end. Technology, though it frequently begins as a means, invariably forces a more candid and conscious discussion about ends. Technology does not just express exciting values. The accelerated pace of technological change never allows us to rest secure on the values we cherished last year or the ends we selected last month. Goals and values must from now on always be in flux, always in process of reexamination.

Arend van Leeuwen represents a new breed of theologians, a breed which seems to thrive in Holland. For some reason, the Netherlands has produced in recent years a new style in theology, a style which admixes traditional theology, history of religion, sociology and cultural analysis in a manner which makes purists on all sides tremble. But the Dutch are right and the purists wrong. Theology today must be radically contextual, boldly addressing a particular contemporary situation and utilizing the rich tradition of Biblical faith to illuminate and deepen our understanding of the issue. This task van Leeuwen undertakes with relish and with consummate skill. His book not only calls us, as the ancient prophets did, to reexamine the path we are treading and to be aware of other options. It also demonstrates that if the Biblical faith is understood creatively and its insights are brought to bear on the issues which confront us today, that tradition itself seems a lot less dead than we have recently been told.

We live in an age of programming, projection and prediction. Many of the new computerized techniques of entrail examination or oracle consulting move dangerously close to a semi-fatalistic view of history. The truth is that so long as man is man, he is free to change and, as the Bible says, to repent. He can defy trends, baffle expert predictions, deflect statistical projections. But he will do so only when he hears a word which both frees him for history and calls him to responsibility for the future. Arend van Leeuwen has sounded such a call. We may still have time to answer it and to harness technology for human fulfillment rather than allow it to reduce us to ciphers. In issuing this call, van Leeuwen has himself become a bit of a prophet.

H. G. C.

Cambridge, Massachusetts
September 1967

▣   Introduction

Does this technocratic era of ours still leave room for
genuine prophecy? Of course, our time is not lacking
heroic voices protesting against a fateful course of events
or foretelling doom and catastrophe unless human history will make a radical turn. In various parts of the
world we meet men possessed by a burning desire for
righteousness whose struggles against the absurdities of
the traditional order sometimes assume prophetic features. It is true that real prophets do not always need
audiences listening to their messages: the lonely desert
with its naked stones and wild animals may even be the
necessary birthplace and the natural milieu of a prophetic spirit.

Nevertheless, neither stones nor animals but human beings living together in a human society are those whom prophecy addresses. And the point at stake is not whether there are in our modern world still deserts as escapes for prophets but whether civilization itself has not turned into a real desert. Whatever one's exact definition of prophecy may be, it will by all means contain two indispensable characteristics: it is directed toward an open future and it appeals to the possibility of conversion. Where these two conditions are missing, what remains is the realm of sheer necessity. Prophecy is incompatible with any kind of determinism, no matter whether of an optimistic or a pessimistic character. Whereas unavoidable decline and ultimate catastrophe is the prospect of pessimism, an optimistic approach may conceive of the course of history as continuous progress. In both cases the dialectical relationship between the freedom of history and man's freedom has been replaced by the automatism of a causal nexus or the dictate of an unescapable order.

TECHNOLOGICAL DETERMINISM

A deterministic approach to the technocratic era is, to be sure, hardly avoidable. The very structure of the technological order possesses a logical strictness and a rational self-evidence which seem to sterilize the tender seeds of freedom. There appears to be a chance for freedom to grow only outside of the technocratic reign or within the few oases existing in the technocratic desert. A striking specimen of an approach which comes very close to a deterministic concept is found in the thinking of the French Protestant scholar Jacques Ellul.[1]

"Technique," thus goes a definition of Ellul, "has become the new and specific *milieu* in which man is required to exist, one which has supplanted the old *milieu*, viz. that of nature." This definition, though still susceptible to various interpretations, has in itself a strong tendency toward a deterministic concept. The very idea that technique should replace nature emerges from a dualistic philosophy in which man as subject finds himself in principle opposed to nature as object. One might wonder how technique may become the genuine heir and successor to nature without having altered fundamentally the character of nature's reign and of its relationship to the domain of man.

Ellul's description of the technical milieu begins by pointing to its artificial character. This recognition could be the starting point for reflecting upon the basic contradiction between the milieu of nature and the milieu of technique, to demonstrate that over against the realm of nature which exists prior to and independently of man's existence, the technical domain is man's own creation. Thus technique, as a man-made phenomenon which replaces nature, encroaches upon the independent essence of the natural order and cannot, for that reason, be meaningfully approached by a dual-

[1] Jacques Ellul, *The Technological Society*, trans. by John Wilkinson (New York, 1964) (originally in French: *La technique ou l'enjeu du siecle*, 1954). Cf. "The Technological Order," article of J. Ellul in: *The Technological Order, Proceedings of the Encyclopaedia Britannia Conference* (Detroit, 1963), pp. 10–38.

istic concept. Technical man and technical milieu are mutually involved to an extent which simply overturns the subject-object-contradiction.

This is, however, not the conclusion drawn by Ellul. To the contrary, his basic thesis is rooted in the appalling discovery that the technical milieu has not only supplanted the natural milieu but has inherited the unchanged object-character of nature. The technical milieu is autonomous in regard to values and ideas, and the state.[2] It is self-determining, a closed circle. Like nature, it is a closed organization which permits it to be self-determinative independently of all human intervention. It grows according to a process which is causal but which is not directed toward ends. It is formed by an accumulation of means which have established primacy over ends. And, as a final characteristic, all its parts are mutually implicated to such a degree that it is impossible to separate them or to settle any one technical problem in isolation.

It follows from this concept that man, up to the present, has been capable neither of giving direction and orientation to technique nor of mastering it. The values spoken of in the technological society are simply there to justify what is, or they are generalities without consequence, or technical progress realizes them auto-

[2] In an address to the World Conference on Church and Society, held by the World Council of Churches in Geneva, 1966, Ellul formulated it this way: "We cannot say 'it is very good' nor 'it is very bad'." That has no meaning; it is like saying that a great flowing river is good or bad. We simply have to confirm an actual fact: technology is expanding, and it is impossible to stop it or to change its course."

matically as a matter of course. For the same reason, a new civilization cannot appear which is inclusive of technique. The transition from the technically quantitative to the humanly qualitative civilization is impossible. Technical power leads to a growth of limitless power which makes values disappear. And, though it frees mankind from a whole collection of ancient constraints, the operation of technique is the contrary of freedom: it is an operation of determinism and necessity.

Is not there a counter-force to be found in man's moral and religious tendencies? No, says Ellul, for as technique produces a new technological morality, it also tends to absorb potential conflicts and to integrate instinctive and religious forces by giving them a place within its structure. This may happen by an adaptation of Christianity or by the creation of new religious expressions, new myths and mystiques that are fully compatible with the technological society (Communism would be such an instance).

The problem posed by this deterministic approach to modern technique seems hardly solvable. Some authors hold that the problem will solve itself; others hold that the problem demands a great effort or even a great modification of the whole man. But all these solutions appear to repose on a too superficial and a too optimistic view of the technical phenomenon. Ellul himself does not pretend to give any solution: what he does claim to be is capable of indicating some *necessary* conditions for a possible solution. The most essential condition consists in ruthlessly destroying the "myth" of technique, i.e. the whole ideological construction and the tendency to consider technology as something possessing sacred character.

So surprising a conclusion seems to contradict the initial thesis of this author. On one hand, Ellul has been the first to produce a "myth" of technique by comparing the technical milieu with the milieu of nature, as if both milieus belong to the same category. On the other hand, his pertinent declaration that technique is a closed circle which absorbs all critical values and ideas has from the very outset eliminated any potential force which might save us from the "myth" of technique. It is his conviction that technique produces its own myth. Ellul proclaims an "authentic philosophy of real meaning" (in opposition to the sterile philosophical preoccupation with "semantics") as the saving mediation between man and the technical phenomenon, but it is difficult to see what this means. For either this philosophy is part of the technical milieu and is, in that case, hopelessly integrated and deprived of its critical spirit; or it is an irrelevant philosophy, rooted in values and categories which technique already has made obsolete. The same dilemma tends to sterilize the necessary dialogue which could represent the "*permanent* and *basic* confrontation between technique's pretensions to resolve all human problems and the human will to escape technical determinism" that Ellul proposes.

There is in Ellul's approach a basic contradiction between the fundamental thesis of the *reality* of technical determinism as belonging to the very essence of the technical phenomenon and the conclusion that man can escape technical determinism and has the calling to do so. It is difficult to imagine that this kind of "escape" is, in last instance, different from the idealistic escape from the material realm into the realm of the pure spirit.

FIGHTING EXISTENTIAL NAUSEA

Ellul's philosophy fails to present any solution to the problem posed by technique because it is based on a wrong diagnosis. To be sure, there does exist something like a "myth" of technique and this myth has, indeed, a pseudo-messianic pretension of possessing the ultimate key to all problems. Another philosopher of technological civilization, Dennis Gabor, summons us to fight the existential nausea which may be the unavoidable outcome of unhalted technological progress.[3] The dogma of growth is continuously stimulating a "whirling dervish economy," to which all governments, capitalist and communist, are committed. At some time, however, this insane growth must be stopped: exponential curves grow to infinity only in mathematics. Compared to what this operation will be, the slowing down of a spaceship with retrorockets is child's play. The very hint of an approaching phase of saturation and stagnation will create apathy and depression—"unless by that time we shall possess a new ethic." In an age of leisure, the basis of the Protestant ethic that glorifies the value of strenuous labor will be destroyed. Nevertheless, even more

[3] Dennis Gabor, "Fighting Existential Nausea" in: *Technology and Human Values*, pub. by the Center for the Study of Democratic Institutions (Santa Barbara, California, Sept. 1966), pp. 13–18.

than a trained intelligence, the technological society requires man to exhibit ethical values. But what are they? Although we know fairly precisely what is meant by "intelligence," we have only a vague concept of "ethical values." Dennis Gabor looks for the answer by designing an "ethical quotient" (E.Q.), a scale for measuring behavior, which he believes is as necessary to characterize the social usefulness of a person as the I.Q.

The concept of a new ethics relevant to a technological society seems promising. Upon looking at the sample of such an ethical scale, however, one wonders whether it has anything to do with real ethics. In fact, Gabor's scale comes down to a traditional list of—as he calls it—"characteristics of social behavior"; it is an "objective" scale of deeds that ignores entirely whether socially useful behavior is motivated by the active love of fellow-brethren, by unconscious inhibition, by vanity, by the fear of the police, by the fear of God, or by the love of God. Gabor states that the "assessment of merit" which takes into account such an evaluation "would be a matter for theologians rather than for social scientists."

This is a significant acknowledgment! It is difficult to see how a social scientist can dismiss the question of whether the human behavior which he conceives as "social" is inspired by spontaneous love of fellow-brethren or by the fear of the police. The kind of theology willing to accept the design of an E.Q. that leaves to social science the discrimination between "social" and "anti-social" behavior is even more questionable. Such social science and such a theology have ignored the decisive problem. The point at issue is that a technological society, being capable of integrating to the point of absorption all non-technological values and ideals, sets a high premium on that type of "social behavior" which identifies itself with the structuring, the direction, and the goals of technological society. Quite possibly this self-evident conformism is the actual source of that appalling "existential nausea" which Dennis Gabor fears as one of the gravest dangers of that society. But if this is true, then an effective fight against this threat has to begin with turning upside-down the very scale of ethical behavior which he considers a starting point of that campaign. The most creative remedies against this "nausea" (actions, therefore, that would merit the highest grading of E.Q.) would have to be produced by a people who refused to act in conformity with the pattern of technological society. The matter, then, is one not only of inner motivations but of social behavior in relation to the total social structure: it is a question that concerns social scientists no less seriously than theologians.

DOOMSDAY MACHINE

An adequate "ethical" or "human" approach to the dilemma of technological society is not easily attained. It may be worthwhile to turn for a third test case to a special field of modern technology, namely to that of modern weapons-systems. Herman Kahn has devoted a penetrating study to the dilemmas of the present arms race.[4] In the opinion of many experts and laymen, the

[4] Herman Kahn, "The Arms Race and Some of Its Hazards" in *Arms Control, Disarmament, and National Security,* ed. by Donald G. Brennan (New York, 1960), pp. 89ff.

best method of preventing the potential causes of war from actually causing a war is to procure what are called "stable deterrent systems." It is desirable that a deterrent should be frightening, inexorable, persuasive, cheap, and non-accident-prone. In order to illustrate the implications of a maximal deterrent system, Kahn describes the conceptualized device of a "Doomsday Machine." The function of this device is to destroy the world. It is protected from enemy action (perhaps by being situated thousands of feet underground) and then connected to a computer, in turn connected to thousands of sensory devices all over the United States. The computer would be programmed so that if, say, five nuclear bombs exploded over the United States, the device would be triggered and the world destroyed.

Logically speaking, this type of "ideal deterrent" would be the adequate technological answer to the challenges of technological progress in the field of armament. It meets exactly the five above mentioned requirements: frightening, inexorable, persuasive, cheap, and foolproof. The difficulties lie, however, in the fact that it lacks a sixth indispensable quality: the Doomsday Machine is not sufficiently *controllable*. In case of a failure, too many people would be killed, and they would be killed too automatically. Even if we abandoned the computer, and made the device reliably controllable by the decision-makers, probably no big power would be willing to give a few individuals this particular kind of life-and-death power over the entire world.

If this "maximal" solution is not feasible, there remain "certain awkward questions" which Kahn forces both policy-maker and technician to consider. The decisive question is this: if it is not acceptable to risk the lives of the *three billion* inhabitants of the earth in order to protect ourselves from surprise attack, then *how many people would we be willing to risk?* His own suggestion is that both the United States and the North Atlantic Treaty Organization would reluctantly envisage the possibility of one or two hundred million fatalities from the immediate effects (the long-term effects due to radiation not included), and this for "moral and political reasons." The main reason, however, the Soviet Union and the United States would not build a Doomsday Machine is that "they are both *status quo* powers."

TECHNOLOGY AND ETHICS

We, then, meet here a remarkably conceptualized position revealing the unescapable obligation for politicians and technologians to face ethical questions. In the name which Kahn has invented for this hypothetical device the full paradox of present technology is tersely summarized. Doomsday, which up to the present time has always been the symbol of the ultimate and absolute powerlessness of mankind to shape its own fate, is now literally being laid in man's own hands or, to put it better, in the power of a machine and of a series of computers that react automatically. The machine is a technical possibility but nonetheless it has not been built and probably will never be built, Kahn hazards, solely for "moral and political reasons." To be a *status quo* power has, in this case, the sole meaning of respecting a certain margin of risk, of refusing to risk global suicide, of acknowledging a basic quality which has aptly been characterized as "survival ethics."

This third sample of a possible concept of the relationship between technology and ethics throws a revealing light upon the cases represented by Ellul's and Gabor's views. "What we dare not face is not total extinction, but total meaninglessness." If this statement of David Riesmann is true, then the gravest problem of technological society does not exist at the bottom (namely the capacity of committing global suicide), but at the top. On the other hand, the danger for mankind to commit suicide is incomparably more acute than the nightmare of a universal but nauseatingly limitless abundance. This might be an indication that technological society, when it comes face to face with the question of sheer survival, reveals a capacity of giving preponderance to "moral and political" reasons prior to the so-called "technical necessity." It is at this point that a supposed technological determinism evidently does not exist and is revealed as being part of the "myth" produced by technological society. If this is the case at the bottom, why should it be *essentially* different (although doubtless different in quality) at the top? The traditional dualism of which Ellul's and Gabor's positions are outstanding specimens is a fundamentally inadequate starting point for analyzing the dilemma of technological society, let alone for remedying its diseases.

SCIENCE AND POLITICS

Herbert Marcuse has argued in favor of a reversal of the traditional relationship between science and metaphysics.[5] The historical achievement of science and technology has rendered possible the *translation of values into technical tasks*—the materialization of values. The new ends, as technical ends, would then operate in the projection and in the construction of the machinery, and not only in its utilization. Moreover, the new ends might assert themselves even in the construction of scientific hypotheses—in pure scientific theory. From the quantification of secondary qualities, science would proceed to the quantification of values. Under this aspect, "neutral" scientific method and technology become the science and technology of a historical phase which has reached its determinate negation. Instead of being separated from science and left to subjective preference, ideas of human liberation formerly considered metaphysical may become the proper object of science.

However, thus Marcuse's significant conclusion, this development confronts science with the unpleasant task of becoming *political*—of recognizing scientific consciousness as political consciousness, and the scientific enterprise as political enterprise. Science and technology would *pass beyond* the stage at which they were, because of their neutrality, *subjected* to politics and were

[5] Herbert Marcuse, *One-Dimensional Man: Studies in the Ideology of Advanced Industrial Society* (Boston, 2d print, 1966), pp. 231ff.

functioning, against their intent, as political instrumentalities. To the extent that technology has developed on this basis, the correction can never be the result of technical progress *per se*. It involves a political reversal.

This political reversal transcends the present conflict between different political systems or ideologies and lays the axe at the root of *all* technological fetishism, exhibited, for instance, in ideas of the future omnipotence of technological man. Technology, as a universe of instrumentalities, may increase the weakness as well as the power of man. At the present stage, he is perhaps more powerless over his own apparatus than he ever was before. The mystification of the idea of a "technological Eros" is not removed by transferring technological omnipotence from particular groups to the new state and the central plan.

AUTOMATION

An illustrative example is the advanced stage of technical progress, represented by *automation*. It is suggested by Marcuse that expanding automation is more than quantitative growth of mechanization—it is a change in the character of the basic productive forces.[6] Automation appears to be the great catalyst of advanced industrial society: once it became *the* process of material production, it would revolutionize the whole society. Complete automation in the realm of necessity would open the dimension of free time as the one in which man's private *and* societal existence would constitute it-

[6] Marcuse, pp. 35ff.

self. This would be the historical transcendence toward a new civilization. Automation seems to be incompatible with a society based on the private exploitation of human labor in the process of production. But it is no less questionable whether it is compatible with the communist system in its established forms. Certainly, by the power of total administration, automation in the Soviet system can proceed more rapidly once a certain technical level has been attained. But the actual development in present-day communist society postpones the qualitative change to the second phase of the disappearance of the State, the Party, the Plan, etc., and the transition from capitalism to socialism appears, in spite of the revolution, still as a quantitative change. If, however, automation could lead to self-determination at the very base of human existence, namely in the dimension of necessary labor, it would be "the most radical and most complete revolution in history."

Marcuse is not alone in making this kind of a far-reaching statement about the consequences of automation, but his voice is surrounded by a choir of experts who, for all the diversity of their evaluations, agree upon the novelty of the impact of automation. A few illustrations might suffice.[7]

It is my thesis that machines can and do *transcend* some of the limitations of their designers, and that in doing so they may be both effective and dangerous. . . . Though machines are theoretically subject to

[7] The following quotations are from articles reprinted in *Automation, Implications for the Future*, ed. Morris Philipson (New York: Vintage Books, 1962). Italics are mine.

human criticism, such criticism may be *ineffective* until long after it is relevant. . . . This leaves us the much more directly *moral question*: What are the moral problems when man as an individual operates in connection with the controlled process of a much slower time scale, such as a portion of *political history* or—our main subject of inquiry—the *development of science?* . . . If we adhere simply to the creed of the scientist, that an incomplete knowledge of the world and of ourselves is better than no knowledge, we can still *by no means* always justify the naive assumption that the faster we rush ahead to employ the new powers for action which are opened up to us, *the better* it will be. We must always exert the *full strength of our imagination to* examine where the full use of our *new modalities* may lead us.

NORBERT WIENER[8]

The definition of *man's uniqueness* has always formed the Kernel of his *cosmological and ethical systems.* . . . As we begin to produce mechanisms that think and learn, he has ceased to be the species uniquely capable of complex, intelligent manipulation of his environment. I am confident that man will, as he has in the past, find a new way of describing *his place in the universe*—a way that will satisfy his needs for dignity and for purpose. But it will be a way *as different* from the present one *as was the Copernican* from the Ptolemaic.   HERBERT A. SIMON[9]

I believe that of all electronic inventions now within viewing distance *predictors* are likely to have the great-

[8] From "Some Moral and Technical Consequences of Automation," printed in *Science*, May 6, 1960.

[9] From "The Corporation: Will It Be Managed by Machines?" in *Management and Corporation: 1985,* eds. Anshen & Bach (New York, 1961).

est influence on civilization. . . . A false and irresponsible predictor like Hitler *can ruin a civilization;* in fact we have now reached the stage when we cannot afford another Hitler. . . . The machine, being a learning machine, will soon notice that everything it says goes, and from that moment on there is no guarantee against its going astray. *Absolute power will corrupt not only men but also machines!* Let us hope that these things will be better understood before social predictors become important.

DENNIS GABOR[10]

We make and solve our own problems chiefly by *other than mathematical logical standards,* and so must *the cybernated generation.* What these standards might be, we do not know. But if they are inadequate, the frustration and pointlessness that they produce may well evoke, in turn, *a war of desperation.* . . . One thing is clear: if the new "logic" is to resolve the problems raised here, it will have to generate *beliefs, behaviour and goals far different* from those which we have held until now and which are driving us more and more inexorably into a contradictory world run by (and for?) ever more intelligent, ever more versatile slaves.   DONALD N. MICHAEL[11]

The predictable part of the future may be a job for electronic predictors, but that part of it which is *not predictable,* which is largely a matter of free human choice, is not the business of machines nor of scientists, not even of psychologists, but it ought to be, as it was in the great epochs of the past, the prerogative

[10] From "Inventing the Future," printed in *Encounter,* May, 1960.

[11] From "Cybernation: The Silent Conquest," a Report to the Center for the Study of Democratic Institutions (Santa Barbara, California, 1962).

of the inspired humanists, of the poets and writers. And for more than a generation we receive from these quarters little else but more or less polished expressions of *despair and disgust*.   DENNIS GABOR[12]

The challenge of automation cannot be faced by looking to the past. . . . Automation will present us with increasing problems. The solutions to those problems . . . will require courage, determination and above all a willingness to blaze new trails . . . if automation is not to become *an unguided monster* leaving hardship and suffering where it passes by, but a tool which we can use to create abundance for all.
          WALTER P. REUTHER[13]

Most, if not all, of man's inventions are instrumentalities which may be employed *by both saints and sinners*. . . . If we *believe*, as *most scientists* do, that it is in our advantage to increase the rate at which we can acquire knowledge, then we can hardly do otherwise than to assert that the modern digital computer is a modality whose value is *overwhelmingly on the side of the good*.   ARTHUR L. SAMUEL[14]

Our culture still has a strong inclination to measure the importance of identity . . . by the importance to a system of the operations which someone is performing. As automation progresses, more and more of the systems in which men function and from which they seek importance will be seen to be automatic systems, allowing no importance to the individuality of their parts. Automation may well produce *a revolution in*

[12] From "Inventing the Future," *Encounter*, May, 1960.
[13] From Testimony Submitted to the Sub-Committee on Automation and Energy Resources, 86th Congress, Second Session.
[14] From "Some Moral and Technical Consequences of Automation—A Refutation," printed in *Science*, September 16, 1960.

*our culture's ways of measuring importance of iden-
tity.*   EDWARD T. D. CALHOUSE[15]

Automation is little more than a projection into the
economic sphere of *philosophical beliefs* that have become dominant in the past fifty years. . . . It might,
with considerable over-simplification, be called an *organic philosophy.* . . . The *Automation Revolution*
is here, and it is proceeding at high speed. . . . Automation is *not technocracy* under another name . . .
it is a concept of the structure and order of economic
life, the design of its basic patterns integrated into a
harmonious, balanced and organic whole.
                             PETER F. DRUCKER[16]

We have here a major explanation of the phenomenon of the so-called *Beat Generation.* They illustrate
the pattern of work and leisure when one of the terms
has vanished: they are *only at leisure.* To me they
seem . . . to be *rich and poignant with history.* For
they *celebrate the unfulfilled promise of the American
Revolution,* the failure of the French Revolution and
the Revolution of 1848, the betrayal of the Russian
Revolution and the fizzling out of our Sit-Downs.
                             PAUL GOODMAN[17]

The task for the sixties will be to hurdle or *push
aside the social and political barriers* which in the past
have prevented American society from progressing on
the social plane at a rate commensurate with its technical progress. Certainly the knowledge and experi-

[15] From "Why Machines Will Never Think," printed in
Automation, Implications for the Future, ed. Morris Philipson.
[16] From "The Promise of Automation," printed in *Harper's
Magazine,* April 1955.
[17] From "The Mass Leisure Class," printed in *Esquire,* July
1959.

ence to do this is at hand: *if the social and political will are forthcoming.*   EVERETT M. KASSALOW[18]

The real point of all this is not that thinking machines are going to become the masters of men, but rather that men must think out quite carefully—and *quite soon*—what they want the machines to do and *how the machines are to be fitted into the social fabric without painful rents and tears.* DAVID BERGAMINI[19]

To my mind, there is a clear need for *national policy* aimed at making the most effective use of technological change.   JOHN DIEBOLD[20]

The potential of the machines for *big-brother prying* is certainly great. . . . Whether the computers' latent ability to run a nation with a tight, efficient hand is ever used in the United States depends on *political decisions* still to be made.   DAVID BERGAMINI[21]

SECULAR PROPHECY

There is in these statements, for all their great variety, a remarkable unison of dramatic overtones, particularly evident within the italicized phrases. The technological trend which has become familiar as the "automation revolution" is apparently opening up depth-

[18] From "Labor Relations and Employment Aspects After Ten Years [1962]," printed in *Automation,* ed. Morris Philipson.

[19] From "Government by Computers," printed in *The Reporter,* August 17, 1961.

[20] From Congressional Testimony Submitted to the Sub-Committee on Automation and Energy Resources, 86th Congress, Second Session.

[21] From "Government by Computers."

dimensions of human existence and is conjuring up decisions which are to determine the future of human society. This is a fine illustration of what is hinted at in our title "Prophecy in a Technocratic Era." The "prophetic" overtone which is to be heard in most of these statements does not arise out of any deliberate theological or ethical approach but it emerges, so to speak, from an analysis and evaluation of factual technological realities.

What is, in this context, the exact meaning of the term "prophetic"? Is the term at all definable without a strict reference to the Bible? One might, for instance, propose as a minimum condition for a truly prophetic attitude that it contains, in some way or another, a recognizable witness to the Word of God. The problem is that this norm may be completely correct and at the same time may be completely void of concrete meaning. And it is the very sting of biblical prophecy which is directed against this type of fallacy (see, for instance, Jeremiah 7: 3f.; Matthew 7: 21ff.). Even the most detailed and exact description of the features of biblical prophecy might not make the slightest contribution to an understanding of prophecy in our own era. What is decisive is a discernment of the deep currents under the surface of modern cultural and social trends. With a reference to Immanuel Kant's formula concerning the meaninglessness of either mere abstract concepts or mere concrete perception, the dilemma might be summarized as follows: "biblical" prophecy, in isolation, is void, whereas "secular" prophecy, in isolation, is blind. Probably there is in a lot of "secular" prophecy a genuine, though implicit, sensitivity to those realities which a good deal of explicit witness to the name of the Lord is trying in vain to disclose. It may be a test case for the truly biblical contemporary prophecy whether it is able to recognize this sensitivity in the "secular" prophetic voices of our time.

A PRO-WESTERN BIAS?

A closing remark may be useful to prevent a grave misunderstanding which might be aroused by the following chapters. This is the idea that some kind of pro-western bias may have confused my mind. I am fully aware of running the risk of this type of accusation or suspicion. I would have preferred to avoid this danger, but I don't see a way. At the very moment one claims for western civilization, particularly in its present "technocratic" stage, some kind of uniqueness, one gets exposed to this objection. Apparently the resistance is only aggravated if I suggest that a connection exists between this unique character of modern science and technology on one hand and the unique quality of biblical "theocracy" on the other. It is much simpler to deny both this uniqueness and its relationship to the historical roots of Christianity. In fact, I don't believe in a simplicity which is only apt to touch the surface and which very probably will deprive us of a chance to penetrate into the core of the deeper question.

Personally, I have not the slightest inclination to defend, let alone to justify or to glorify, western civilization. A mere reference to the fact that the threat of global suicide for our generation results from recent progress of western science and technology might be sufficient to smother any tendency in that direction. But the point at stake is not whether modern technocracy is a blessing or a curse: it is both. And we do not have the choice between judging or praising the results of modern science, for we have to do both. The real issue is the undeniable and inescapable reality of technocracy which has emerged in the course of western civilization and is now on its way to planetary expansion, destined to affect radically the way of living of the *whole* of mankind. Modern technocracy is a historical phenomenon. Certainly the time will come when this phenomenon will have assumed such a truly planetary extension and will have so radically unified mankind's civilization that reference to its historical origin in the preceding stage of western civilization may be like hinting at some "pre-historical" stage. May that time come soon! For at that time it will be possible to raise the questions I have tried to bring to the surface, without getting entangled into an inextricable net of emotional reactions against a supposed "western-crusading" mentality.

The heart of the matter does not lie in the origins of our technocratic era, in its past, but it consists in its destiny, in its future. Only a truly prophetic approach will be adequate to answer the challenge of our technocratic destination.

O N E

▣ Prophecy and Technocracy

SOME PRELIMINARY REMARKS

The world-wide cooperative mission and service obligation of the churches focuses on the calling of the laity in mission. This role could be pithily summed up as "prophecy in a technocratic era." Prophecy and technocracy are the two focuses of the elliptic shape of the general theme of this book.

Prophecy is the fundamental criterion for our Christian existence in the present world. The crucial distinction is neither between clergy and laity, or between theology and secular science, nor between word and deed, or between mission and service, but between *prophetic* and *unprophetic* theology, laity, mission, service, etc. Moreover, the term "prophetic" has the ad-

36

vantage of embracing three qualities: it has a long tradition, it is radical, and it is comprehensive.

a. Prophecy is firmly rooted in the tradition of the Old Testament: there runs a prophetic line through the history of church and Christianity from the beginning until the present time.

b. The prophet is the radical critic of his own people, of the elected nation, of church and Christianity. He witnesses to the judgment which begins in the house of God.

c. In spite of his lonely position, the prophet has a vicarious role on behalf of the whole people of God. He links up present, past, and future by continuing the prophetic Word of the past, presenting it to his own generation, and discerning the signs of the coming Kingdom. Prophecy, then, is comprehensive.

Technocracy is a keyword to the situation of modern society and culture. The term combines two characteristics:

a. Technology as the principal fruit of modern science, and, for this reason, the visible "face" of abstract knowledge and mathematical concepts.

b. The suffix "-cracy" points to the structural and societal aspect of the achievements of modern science. Technology is not only applied science, but it determines our way of life and the character of our planetary development.

Between the criteria of prophecy and of technocracy there is strong tension. The biblical and Christian tradition of prophecy meets, in the technocratic era, an unprecedented situation which represents not only an accidental, but a fundamental, challenge to the whole prophetic tradition. Be it said that technocracy is far more than a simple sociological or cultural fact; it is the outcome of a unique evolution of western Christian civilization and it is indissolubly connected with a deep-rooted though, more often than not, veiled secular faith in man's capacity and calling to transform nature and to humanize our existence. It is this very faith which constitutes a profound challenge to the traditional understanding of prophecy.

Both terms are the mutually opposite focuses of *one* elliptic whole which is both the condition and the continuous creator of the tensions. The basic issue for church and mission in the second half of our century is how to stay within (or to enter) this magnetic field of necessary tensions, how to discern, and how to bear them.

TWO PROPHETS OF THE 20TH CENTURY

In many places of the world two anniversaries were celebrated recently, of John Mott's birth a century ago, and of Dietrich Bonhoeffer's martyr's death on the ninth of April, 1945. Mott died at a mature age, having completed all his tasks and having watched the harvest of his sowing; Bonhoeffer's life was cut off in a concentration camp, before the great future which certainly lay ahead of him was fulfilled—Mott, the nineteenth-century pioneer who planted the vision of nineteenth-century revivalist optimism and evangelistic zeal in the soil of our century; Bonhoeffer, born in the twentieth century, who decided to return to his country just before the Second World War, to share the horrible depths of sin, despair, and suffering of his own people—on one side the American layman, bristling with an expansionist optimism; on the other hand the European theologian, facing the demonic possibilities of our technocratic era. Over against the message of "evangelization of the world in this generation" there stands the surgeon-like analysis of a "world come of age" and the appeal to a "religionless Christianity." There was perhaps more than accidental significance in the fact that in one year the birth of one and the death of the other were commemorated.

The theme "prophecy in a technocratic era" might be wonderfully illustrated by the coincidence of their double anniversary. I myself have to confess my great indebtedness to both. Church and missions on the continent of Europe owe much to the inspiration of the magnificent tradition which has interpreted John Mott's vision all over the world and which still remains the continuous source of the mainstream of American missions and world service. But I should not be honest if I did not reveal that the deepest stirrings of my soul are touched when I read and reread the unforgettable pages of Bonhoeffer's *Letters from Prison*. Not only because I am, like him, a continental theologian, not only on account of the deep incision which for my generation the German occupation and the terrors of Nazism have produced, but also because I feel in Bonhoeffer's approach a prophetic sensitiveness of things to come and a radical

insight in the definitive break, resulting from the Second
World War, in a still, up to that time, unbroken tradition. Mott and Bonhoeffer both deserve the name of
prophet, but between them there is a chasm. It is exactly this chasm which to bridge in our thinking and in
our acting is our common Christian calling.

TWO SECULAR PROPHECIES

We should fall short of a realistic sketch of the
implications of our theme if we only look to Christian
prophets of our time. There is in our time, as the other
side of the medal, also a type of secular prophecy; or
better, there are several and even contradictory specimens of secularized prophecies. Let us mention two outstanding specimens.

The famous book of the English writer George
Orwell titled *1984* is an impressive vision of a not too
distant future, designed by a prophetic artist. It is very
difficult to see any analogy between this fascinating
modern novel and the forebodings of doom we meet in
the Bible. Nevertheless, Orwell's way of telling the
truth about the inherent logic that is active in the structures of a technocratic society is reminiscent of the
supra-realistic realism which is so characteristic for the
Old Testament prophets. The only word which is definitely lacking in Orwell's forecast is a word of grace
and hope; it is this omission which separates the novelist
from biblical and from Christian prophetic tradition.

There are also quite different attempts to anticipate

the year 1984. In 1964 the English review *New Scientist* published a series of one hundred articles, written by a number of outstanding scientists and technicians, in which each expert on his specific field of knowledge tried to sketch an outline of the developments in the two decennia ahead of us. The general mood of this symposium (published in 1965 in two volumes of the Penguin Books) is amazingly different from Orwell's conclusions. Over against the unremitting pessimism of the artist-novelist, what we meet here is, in spite of a few exceptions, a self-evident and unreflected optimism about the near future of our technocratic world. Only once or twice—and that hidden in a marginal remark —is the image of continuous and accelerated progress conditioned by the provision that mankind will achieve continuous and accelerated progress only if it is able to escape from atomic suicide. The technologians and the technocrats of our time chiefly tell us about a triumphant future.

There is in their prognoses not even the remotest reminiscence of prophetic insight: there is no pretension whatever in this direction. These scientists and technical experts only try to be as exact as possible about probable developments. Nevertheless, there is behind these forecasts a hidden faith that this trend has an absolutely unresistible character and that it should be continued in the same direction.

The "must" of a self-evident determinism goes hand in hand with the "ought" of a silent optimism. A Christian prophecy which does not come to grips with this over-arching faith of our technocratic world will never manage to address modern man in the language of our time.

A MANIFOLD REVOLUTION

Secular prognoses, like Orwell's book on one hand and this scientific symposium on the other hand, are also delusory to the degree that they overlook the revolutionary consequences of a technocratic development. It is this very aspect that calls for a truly prophetic response, born out of a vision of the fundamentally revolutionary character of human history.

A splendid example of an approach in which diagnosis, prognosis, and therapeutic suggestions are integrated is the report "The Triple Revolution." [1] This statement is written "in the recognition that mankind is at a historic conjuncture which demands a fundamental reexamination of existing values and institutions." It points to the fact that during our time three separate and mutually reinforcing revolutions are taking place:

    a. the cybernation revolution ("A new era of production has begun. Its principles of organization are as different from those of the industrial era as those of the industrial era were different from the agricultural.").

    b. the weaponry revolution ("New forms of weap-

[1] Published by the Center for the Study of Democratic Institutions at Santa Barbara, California, 1965. Also published in *Information Service,* Department of Research, National Council of Churches, May 22, 1965.

onry have been developed which cannot win wars but which obliterate civilization.").

c. the human rights revolution ("A universal demand for full human rights is now clearly evident. It continues to be demonstrated in the civil rights movement within the United States."). Basic to this statement is the conviction about the interaction of these three revolutions. On the background of this insight stands an approach in which (1) the double significance of the term "revolution," i.e. as a critical development on the technological and on the social level, is acknowledged; and (2) the proposals for action bear a comprehensive character.

Therefore, the prophetic style of this report is not merely born out of moral indignation but springs from a scientific analysis of technological changes. In this combination, the statment is a good specimen of "prophecy in a technocratic era."

AMERICA AND THE WORLD REVOLUTION

The English historian Arnold J. Toynbee, in a series of lectures delivered at the University of Pennsylvania in 1961 (published by Oxford University Press, 1962), has launched the thesis that "since 1917, America has reversed her role in the world. She has become the arch-conservative power instead of the arch-revolutionary one. Stranger still, she has made a present of her glorious discarded role to the country which was the arch-conservative power in the nineteenth century, the country which, since 1946, has been regarded by America as being America's Enemy Number One. America has presented her historic role to Russia." Is this reversal of roles America's irrevocable choice, Toynbee wonders. Can America rejoin her own revolution?

> The shot fired beside the bridge at Concord was not only heard around the World; it was taken as a signal, given to the World by the embattled American farmers, that the World Revolution has begun. . . . What, then, is America's relation to the World Revolution? It is her revolution; it was she who launched it by firing the shot heard round the World.

> What about America's recently acquired affluence? It is a handicap, and a formidable one, but it is a handicap that can be overcome. Can America rejoin her own revolution? In my belief, this is still within her power. America's destiny is, I believe, still in America's own hands.

These challenging theses and questions, put forward by a critical friend like Toynbee, should be taken seriously, even if (in my opinion, this is surely the case!) some of his presuppositions and therapeutic counsels are dubious.

IN THE CENTER OF BIBLICAL PROPHECY

A splendid guide at the very start of our way through our theme is the New Testament pericope from Matthew 24:1–14. I offer the following comments:

a. The pericope focuses in vs. 14: evangelization of the "oecumene" as an anticipation of the "telos" (eschatological fulfillment). The fullness of space and of time are indissolubly together.

b. Jesus is prophesying in Jerusalem, which is "killing the prophets" (Matt. 23:37). Nevertheless, Jerusalem is the "home base of world evangelization" (Acts 1:8).

c. Jesus has left the temple which he will never visit again. The temple stands under God's definitive judgment (Matt. 23:38; cf. Jer. 22:5).

d. Jesus is the last prophet, who fulfills the line of Old Testament prophecy, where the lines of kingship and priesthood, of palace and temple, of throne and altar have been cut off.

e. Jesus rejects both a false traditionalism (Matt. 24:1) and a premature apocalypticism (Matt. 24:3, 4, 8).

f. Evangelization is to be accompanied by the rise of false christs (Matt. 24:5) and false prophets (Matt. 24:11). One could even say the rise of false christs will be the unavoidable consequence of evangelization, for without Christ there would not be false christs. Evangelization does not only produce faith but also heresies and antifaith.

g. It is extremely difficult to distinguish between Christ and false christs. That means antifaith and heresy are not only and even not in the first place there where Christians have labeled them, but they are in the heart of Christendom itself. Only a faith which "endures to the end" (vs. 13) is able to discern that God's final judgment—not ours—is decisive.

h. Evangelization will be surrounded by a host of tribulations: wars, famines, earthquakes, etc. All this "must" take place. This "must" is, however, not a blind fate or a natural necessity, but it is being caught up within the "must" of Christ's own suffering (cf. Matt. 16:21).

i. This means that not only wars but also famines and earthquakes are being stripped of their character of fatal necessity which is ascribed to them in pagan religion. They are part of the great drama of God's history with mankind, of which Christ's suffering, death, and resurrection are the center and the revelation of its hidden meaning. As Christ in his resurrection has overcome suffering and death, so these tribulations can and should be met by faith in his power. Evangelization is the proclamation of the final victory over wars, famines, and earthquakes.

j. Jesus' prophecy has this dual character: while rejecting any type of fatalism and determinism, it also refutes any type of optimism which neglects the necessity of suffering.

k. Real prophecy is to be hated by all nations (vs. 9). But before bearing the hate of the nations (goyim, that is, gentiles), this prophecy has to meet the hatred of the chosen nation itself

(Matt. 23:37). Mission does not only start from Jerusalem, but it begins as the prophetic word, spoken to and rejected by Jerusalem!

MISSION "BETWEEN THE TIMES": ESCHATOLOGY AND HISTORY

The preaching of the gospel bears testimony to the coming end of history (Matt. 24:14). But it takes place within and throughout the course of history (Matt. 24:5–13). Therefore we have to bear in mind both the historical and the eschatological aspect of mission.

THE HISTORICAL ASPECT

The Bible, being a unity of Old and New Testament, has a profoundly historical character. The history of the Old Testament embraces a protracted series of centuries. The New Testament is the fulfillment of *that* history, which has a well-defined and limited date (the later history of the ancient Near East) and a definite place (the land of Canaan and surrounding countries of the Near and Middle East). This means also that it has pleased God not only to come in the flesh of His Son, but also to choose a nation with all the implications of human corporate existence: cultural, social, economic, political, etc. A missiology which (as is all too familiar) neglects this concrete historical aspect of biblical history, not only spiritualizes the historical character of the gospel, but it overlooks the fundamentally historical character of missionary history itself. The gospel which is evangelized is not a supra-historical or a-historical "eternal" truth, but the process of evangelization is part of the gospel.

Prophecy in a technocratic era involves the problem of how the gap between biblical history and ours is to be bridged and how biblical prophecy can be translated into the language of modern man. Or, to put it in another way, how can we discern between true and false prophecy, for example, with a view to some specimens of contemporary prophecy which have been presented above. It is obvious, for example, that modern prophecy has to do with concrete political, social, and cultural implications and, particularly, as far as the American church and mission are concerned, with the historical situation which the United States is facing today. Is there a link between modern and biblical prophecy and is there a connection between the particular place and calling of American churches and missions and the particular place and calling of the people of Israel as it is witnessed in the Bible? When American Christians preach the gospel at home and all over the world, their message bears a historical character both on account of their being Americans and of their being Christians. American Christianity of today is, through a long history of evangelization, Christianization, and expansion of the church and of missions, connected with the beginning of missions at Pentecost and with the long history of the Old Testament of which this was the fulfillment.

Nevertheless there is a broad gulf between biblical times and ours, between the United States and the land of Canaan, and it is very dubious whether this gap can be bridged. But, at the same time we should realize that it is the very fact of our historical consciousness which has sharpened our insight in the existence of this hardly bridgeable gap! And the crucial question is whether it is not only our awareness of this distance but the fact of this chasm itself which has resulted in the preaching of the gospel, being an historical act and a witness to the word of God which has become flesh in human history. Our technocratic era is radically different from the type of civilization in which Moses, David, and Daniel, and also Jesus and Paul lived. Should not it be the very task and the capacity of real prophecy to interpret this radical transformation of culture as the ongoing history in which man is being called to take leave of the past and to enter upon the adventure of an "Exodus" which requires the vision of faith and hope? It might be the unprecedented newness of our technocratic era which at the same time brings us into such a flagrant contradiction with the whole biblical context and which on the other hand forces us radically to renew our message of a God who makes all things new, not only within the human soul and not only at the end, but also within the context of cultural and social history.

THE ESCHATOLOGICAL ASPECT

It is precisely this particular history of the people of Israel, taking place within this particular setting of time and place and within this particular social and cultural context, that has at the same time *universal* significance. It is God's dealing with this people that is being witnessed to *all* nations. And it is this Old Testament history that is foreshadowing and anticipating its eschatological fulfillment in the New Testament, looking forward to the New Jerusalem which will be the abiding capital for the coming Kingdom. Therefore, we cannot dismiss this particular character of biblical history as secondary or accidental, for it is the very *raison d'être* of Christian mission that this particular history is being universally proclaimed.

This also affects the historical relationship between Mission in the twentieth century and biblical times. Referring to the particular *place* of American missions, we have to consider the question to what extent and in what respect the particular experiences and opportunities, challenges and handicaps, frustrations and hopes which are part of American history, bear an exemplary character, have a universal meaning, and foreshadow an eschatological future.

Let us mention two examples. Is the fact of the city of New York having become the site of the United Nations Organization a bare historical accident or is it to be seen as an extraordinary privilege and a calling allotted to this nation on account of an extraordinary history? Is the U.N., besides all legitimate skepticism and grave criticism to which it is exposed, also to be looked at as an all-too-human and all-too-frequently-failing attempt to respond to a universal and eschatological vision upon the New Jerusalem for all mankind which from the very outset has been inspiring a series of American pioneers and nation-builders? And should not it be the particular task of American missions to face this historical privilege in a profoundly prophetic way, confronting the "chosen nation" with the extraordinary temptations and opportunities, the unusual dangers and chances, the judgment and hope which are involved in this unique position in present-day history?

As a second example I may refer to the struggle for human rights which is shocking the national existence of the United States to its very foundations. Is not it exactly the universal, primordial, and eschatological creed which has been proclaimed on the birthday of the United States, in its constitutional witness that "all men are created equal" which is the crucial test for this country? The whole world is onlooker in the arena where this struggle is being fought and the outcome of this struggle will have its consequences for the whole of mankind. It is at this point that the name *"United States"* receives still a wider and deeper dimension, referring to the unity of many nations whose emigrants together have built up this country, to the variety of races which together have contributed to its growth, vicariously representing, so to say, in its national body the expected unity of the human race. Should American missions today be realistic without being able to give a prophetic interpretation of the crucial test to which precisely the American nation is being exposed? Are American missionaries only faithful individuals, exporting a timeless message of individual salvation, or are they at the same time and unescapably inhabitants of a nation, passing through an unprecedented trial which reveals its deepest meaning in the light of biblical history? The same holds true in regard to the particular *time* in which American missions are working today.

The United States is the most advanced outpost of modern development; it has already fully entered the period of the "second industrial revolution" and it will, in all probability, be the first nation to introduce new technological revolutions which the future (and, perhaps, some research laboratories already now) keeps in store. Though there is certainly no need for other nations to follow the present-day American way of life, nevertheless the successes and failures of American society in finding solutions for the totally unprecedented challenges of the second industrial revolution will have an exemplary significance for the rest of mankind. Can American missions in "developing" or "underdeveloped" countries be realistic without themselves having prophetically faced the full implications of the technical, cultural, and social revolution which is taking place at home, at the "home base"? Can they really guide members of other nations to God's future when they cannot give an answer with regard to the future of their own society? Or, to say it in other words, can they be really missionary without interpreting their pioneering position in the worldwide evolution of our technocratic age and without exposing it to the light which in biblical history is revealing the eschatological meaning of breaks and crises in human history?

THE CONVERSION OF AMERICA
AND THE CONVERSION OF MANKIND

All this means that becoming a Christian is not the end but is the very beginning of conversion. The term "conversion" should be taken in its truly Old Testament meaning (which is also the Hebrew background of the New Testament term "metanoia"), namely, the return of the chosen people to its Lord whom it had forgotten, to its country from which it has been driven, to its historical mission which it had neglected. Israel could not become a light to the nations and a salt for the whole earth without this return to its genuine place and to the source of its being. We should not forget that the promise of a "New Covenant" first of all refers to the renewal of the covenant "with the house of Israel and the house of Judah" (Jer. 31:31) and that this promise concretely refers to the coming days "when the city shall be rebuilt for the Lord from the tower of Han'anel to the Corner Gate" (Jer. 31:38). To become a Christian means exactly to participate, through Jesus, the Messiah of Israel, in this promise. Certainly, the American nation can by no means replace the people of Israel or repeat its unique historical mission. But on the other hand, not only American individuals but the United States in the totality of its social, cultural, and political structures have been addressed, influenced, and incorporated in an ongoing missionary movement in which this message of the New Covenant has been proclaimed. In other words, the United States of America has more than one dimension:

a. It represents the accidental location of a number of human beings who are God's children whom He calls to conversion.

b. It represents one of the many "nations," the plurality of social groups and corporate structures which in the Old Testament are called *goyim,* in the New Testament *ethne,* in the Latin and English language "gentiles"; more than just a sum of individuals: broken fragments of that primeval "People" which the whole of mankind was united into before their having begun to build the tower of Babel.

c. They are being moulded as a "nation" in the course of western Christian history, unescapably related to the unique example of the "elected nation," the people of Israel which in its privilege and its fall, its heights and its depths, its opportunities and its failures, its pride and its faith, its light and its darkness, holds a mirror to all other "nations," gentiles who have been called to the future of the New Covenant.

A missionary movement that has its "home base" in the United States and which is misinterpreting these dimensions runs the danger of becoming or has already unwittingly become a shadow or a caricature of what Mission really is. It may become one-sidedly individualistic, or it may be turning the gospel into some kind of expansionism of American social ideas and ways of life, or it may degenerate into American zealotism, which pretends to make the world safe for democracy and freedom and to light the candle of American Christendom in a dark world. Or what is more probable, it may become a mixture of these misunderstandings at once.

When American missions have, however, a sound understanding of their role, they will certainly perceive each of these dimensions, separately and together, in a prophetic light: facing each American (and in first instance the missionaries themselves!) (a) with the function of the United States to build, together with all other nations, a human city for the whole of mankind, and (b) with the conversion of America to a radical self-criticism and renewal in the light of the New Covenant.

Mission begins at home. The conversion of mankind starts to the degree that American missions are concerned with the conversion of America. (In the same way, the conversion of the world starts with the conversion of the church!) American missions need not be ashamed to be American; neither should they be hesitant about referring to the full political, economic, cultural, and social implications of this indissoluble relationship. Missionaries are not angels but human beings and missions do not start from the New Jerusalem, neither from the Cross, but from this or that country. The worst missionary illusion is that which tries to forget or hide this earthly reality behind a pious screen of eternal ideas. One may be sure that not only the eye of the Lord but also the eyes of those people who are the object of these missions unremittingly will pierce through this screen. One can better imagine somebody leaping over his own shadow than American missions losing their American character. Therefore the crucial choice is between *prophetic* and *unprophetic* American missions.

T W O

🔲 Secularization and Secularism

SECULARIZATION AS A CHRISTIAN PHENOMENON

The expression "secularization" causes much misunderstanding and confusion. The best definition is that of Friedrich Gogarten: secularization is "the historicization of human life." As such it is the consequence of the Christian faith, which draws a clear distinction between secularization and secularism. In secularization one admits the "creatureliness" of the world. In this, human thought assumes that its own ultimate purpose is to comprehend the universe; at the same time it recognizes its own creaturely limitations, which prevent it from getting any further than a questioning ignorance.

If man cannot bear this paradoxical situation, he falls a victim to secularism, which may assume two different forms. If one passes beyond the limit of nescience

56

and maintains that one can answer the ultimate questions about the universe, this produces the secularism of the modern doctrines-of-salvation and ideologies. On the other hand, if one stops questioning, because one cannot grasp the universe, one is heading for nihilistic secularism. It is the task of the Christian faith to keep secularization on the path of questioning nescience, and to protect it from the menace of ideological or nihilistic secularism.

This clarification of concepts may prevent unnecessary confusion of thought. If one says that the theocracy of Israel under King Solomon, the *Corpus Christianum* in medieval Europe, or the theocracy of classical Islam are "secularized" forms, one means that they had fallen into the secularism of an ideological doctrine of salvation. On the other hand the thesis that the biblical message "secularizes" the world means that the world is liberated from the grip of religious or metaphysical forces and becomes a sphere of creation and history, in which God is leading mankind into His Kingdom. This path which God takes with man is the path of "secularization."

With regard to the two forms of secularism, the ideological and the nihilistic, "secularization" can be described in relation to both these aspects. On the one hand it means a radical "sanctification," because it places everything under the rule of God, the God of Israel and the Father of Jesus Christ. At the same time it means a radical "de-sanctification," because it takes over everything "sacred" in the pagan religions, liberates them from the religious powers, and claims them for the One God. That is why the first Christians were called "atheists" by the Roman authorities. In the history of Christianity we see how "secularization" (in both its aspects) may revert to "secularism."

"Sanctification" develops into Christianization, and in a *Corpus Christianum* this may degenerate into an ideological form of secularism, in which (under a Christian name and with the approval of the church) the old paganism is continued, or reverted to. By freeing life and society from the tyranny of the religious powers, "de-sanctification" may lead to profanation; this finally leads to nihilistic secularism, which sooner or later will appear in ideological form. Where Christianity has become Christian ideology, it arouses the prophetic criticism of the biblical message, which "secularizes" this false form of Christianity. Simultaneously this ideological Christian secularism is directly responsible for the rise of reactionary movements which end in nihilism.

THE CRISIS OF THE TEMPLE

The way in which the biblical message "secularizes" the world is clearly shown in the problems connected with the Temple in the Bible. In all religions the Temple occupies a central position. Only in the Bible the building of the Temple was subject to sharp criticism from the very outset. In the New Testament this criticism culminates in the crucifixion of Jesus, this being the final judgment on the Temple (Matthew 24 and John 2).

The Temple is "made with hands" (cf. Mark 14: 58, Acts 17:24). The Temple, the center of all religion, is criticized because it is nothing more than a piece of ordinary human labor. This has far-reaching conse-quences, which may be illustrated by the symbolic sig-nificance of the Temple.

In all religions the Temple is the symbol of the universe. It is the microcosm, the "Weltbild." The Bible relates that the world was created by the Lord of history. Just as the Children of Israel were led out of Egypt (Exodus) and freed from the tyranny of the pagan religions, so in the same way the world was freed by God's redeeming power from the mythical "Weltall" which He condemns as being "void." Through the power of God the world was "created out of nothingness."

In the New Testament the "cosmos" (which in Greek thought is the eternal, divine universe) becomes the creation which is in travail, awaiting the redemption. The cosmos becomes the sphere of history that God is guiding to its end in Jesus Christ.

The attitude of human thought to the universe is thereby changed, and quite different from the attitude in the pagan religions or in Greek metaphysics. Like the Temple, all the human concepts of the universe are criticized, because they are "made with hands." The mechanization of the "Weltbild" in modern science im-plies a complete rejection of the religious "Weltbild" and of the Greek metaphysical "Weltbild." Modern science has not evolved a new "Weltbild," and it cannot do so as long as it clings to its strictly scientific methods. It can only submit a "sample" which can be used until it is replaced by another sample better adapted to further observation and experiment. This provisional and hypo-thetical character stamps modern science as a purely human activity, going on in history, limited by the "creatureliness" of human thought. When science abandons this path of secularization and regards its "sample" as an infallible metaphysical pronouncement concerning the nature of Reality, it falls a victim to secularism.

The symbol of the Temple is also used in the New Testament (I Cor. 6:19) with regard to the human body. The human body belongs to that category which is described as "made with hands" (cf. II Cor. 5:1). Parallel with the advance of science, and its rejection of the closed, temporal "Weltbild," medical science has penetrated the secrets of the human body, which had eluded all the pagan religions. Even the Greek did not enter into this stage. Modern anatomy begins with vivisection. This revolution took place as the result of a new attitude of western man to reality, which also brought about the fall of the closed medieval social structure. The secularization of medical science may develop into a secularism in which doctors assume that the provisional and partial hypotheses of their knowledge are a complete explanation of what man really is. Or else the doctor may revert to the nihilist position of the "body-technician" who has forgotten to inquire what is the meaning of life, suffering, and death.

Jesus applies the symbol of the Temple to his own body; he is himself the Temple (John 2:21). Jesus' life is thus brought into the category of ordinary humanity, which is "made with hands." Jesus is not "holy" in the general religious sense. On the contrary, his death on the Cross implies a radical de-sanctification (cf. Heb. 13:10–14).

It is therefore not merely permissible, it is essential to study the life of Jesus, and the whole Bible, critically in accordance with the methods of analytical science. As long as this study keeps to the path of secularization, one may be confident that (like all purely scientific work) it will always endeavor to adapt its "sample" to the object to be studied. Just because of our faith in the victorious power of Jesus, the risen Lord, we shall not be afraid to undertake this research. The "history of the research on the life of Jesus" goes further, because it is "research" *and* "history," and in a very special sense, because the subject of its research is the life of Jesus. When this research turns a certain "sample" into an absolute, it is wandering from the path of secularization, and reverting to secularism in one form or another.

In the New Testament the local church is called a "Temple of God" (I. Cor. 3:17). Its "holiness" is different from that of the religious groups. The church is holy in the same way in which its crucified Lord is "holy." It cannot be more than a Temple made with hands, which belongs to this creation (cf. Heb. 9:11). The church is true to its task if it remains on the path of secularization. It reverts to a form of secularism only if it stands in opposition to the world by presuming to possess a Christian ideology, or if it abandons itself to a secular ideology. In actual fact the two things go together, for Christian ideologies always have a secular character concealed within them.

SOME CONSEQUENCES

It is possible to draw some clear conclusions with regard to our attitude (as Christians) to secularization.

a. In secularization we do not encounter anything

strange. It is the fruit of the Bible's message. It is a basic fundamental misconception if the church and Christianity attack secularization. By doing so they are guilty of forcing secularization to revert into secularism. Where they defend themselves against forms of secularism they must make it absolutely clear that they do not want to call people back to a Christian ideology, but to the path of true secularization. People will not believe what the church says unless it takes the path of secularization itself.

b. We urgently need a basic confrontation between theology and secularization. The laity movement within the church betrays the uneasiness which overcomes Christians, when they look in vain to theology for answers to the questions confronting them in a secularized world. Theology will not be able to give adequate answers to these questions until it is "laicized" and "secularized," i.e. until it really determines the way in which "God's people" think and act in the contemporary world.

c. This renewal of theology also involves a fresh confrontation with the sources. Firstly, with the structure of thought in the Bible. Secondly, with the thought of Augustine—not as the basis of a neo-Augustinian system, but as a fresh encounter with a Christian thinker. Augustine, who (like ourselves) lived at a turning-point in history, considered the "historicization" of human life in such a dynamic, bold, and radical way, that both Rome and the Reformation found him a source of inspiration for reflection and reorientation.

Thesis: The great problem for the church is the fact that the basic criticism of its traditional form of expression is now influencing it from outside, by propagating a type of person who applies secularized thought with secularized concepts to nature and man, which have usurped the position and function of God.

God is not "self-evident"; that is the very heart of the biblical revelation. In this it is diametrically opposed to the natural religion of the heathen. Both the Old and the New Testament open by stating that God himself speaks. He is so fathomless as Person, that any attempt to turn Him into an object is impossible, because it would be impossible for thinking man to find a sound ontological basis for it. Nevertheless this attempt is one of the essential signs which distinguish human nature from the rest of the creation. Man is forced into an impossible adventure which (apart from God the Father of Jesus Christ) seems like *hybris,* condemned to tragic failure. Yet in apprehending His revelation man realizes that this adventure is the history of the merciful God Who chooses and judges His people, and the world of nations, and that He will lead that history to its conclusion. This particular apprehension of God drives man to a chronic restlessness, because he has lost the final ontological certainties, and is completely dependent upon God's infinite mercy. Both in the Old and the New Testament, God's people enter the world of nations as irresistible disturbers of the peace, who are constantly being stirred up afresh by the prophetic Word and by the Spirit of God.

In the history of Christian culture in western Europe, this dialectic has culminated in many forms and paradoxical processes. The crisis in security, the influence of atheism and nihilism and "de-Christianization" can be understood only within the setting of this special history. Even in those special cases where a mythical longing for pre-Christian paganism tries to break through, its downfall is overwhelming proof of its impossibility. The church must realize that the criticism (from outside the church) of its traditional form of expression is the repercussion of a long process of Christianization, conducted by itself. The church has conjured up spirits which it is now unable to control. Christianization is an extremely bold enterprise, both when it succeeds and when it fails. But it is simply not possible to continue preaching "the faith," century after century, and at the same time to expect this faith to be accepted as self-evident.

A church which submits nature and man to radical criticism would be sawing off the very branch which shelters it. The breakdown of the *Corpus Christianum* is due to this inner necessity. The history of modern science and the development of modern art, the revolutionary history of western society and politics, reflect the inner conflict, the insoluble dilemma, in which western culture finds itself today, now that the influence of Christian preaching has permeated it, destroying the religious cement which held together the pagan cultures.

Thesis: The church cannot contact this new type of person unless it perceives that he is the product of the church itself, stops regarding such people as a problem for missions "outside the church," and undertakes a thorough theological examination of itself.

One sees what has really conquered the Christian God: it is Christian morality itself, the increasingly strict concept of 'Wahrhaftigkeit,' the scrupulous sensitivity of the Christian conscience translated and sublimated into scientific conscience and intellectual purity. Regarding nature as if it were a proof of the goodness of a protective God; interpreting history so as to honor a divine Reason, as a permanent testimony of a moral order in the cosmos and of ultimate moral purposes; interpreting one's own experience (as pious people have done for long enough) as if everything that happens to one were thought out expressly in order to save one's soul—all that is finished with now. Every sensitive conscience today regards all that as false, weak and cowardly. It is in this severity that we are good Europeans, and heirs of Europe's longest and bravest self-conquest. But while we push this kind of 'Christian' interpretation from us and condemn it as false currency, we are immediately confronted by Schopenhauer's terrible question: 'Then has life any meaning at all?' It will take several centuries even to understand the full implications of that profound question.   FRIEDRICH NIETZSCHE[1]

In a word (and it must be our word of honor!) we are good Europeans, the heirs of Europe, overwhelmed with wealth but at the same time weighed down with

[1] *Die fröhliche Wissenschaft* (Kroner-Verlag, 1940), Book Five, 357.

responsibility due to centuries of the European spirit. As such we have grown out of Christianity and are averse to it . . . just because we have grown out of it, because our forefathers were Christians who were ruthless in their righteous stand for Christianity, and sacrificed their blood and their wealth, their position and their fatherland for the sake of their faith—we do the same. But why? Because of our unbelief? Because of all kinds of unbelief? No, you know better, my friends! The 'Yes' hidden within you is stronger than all the 'Noes' and 'Perhapses' which have made your century sick. If you want to go overseas, you emigrants, it is a *faith* which compels you! . . .

FRIEDRICH NIETZSCHE[2]

The only way to be honest is to recognize that we have to live in the world *etsi deus non daretur*. And this is just what we do see—before God! So our coming of age forces us to a true recognition of our situation vis-à-vis God. God is teaching us that we must live as men who can get along very well without Him. The God who is with us is the God who forsakes us (Mark 15:34). The God who makes us live in this world without using Him as a working hypothesis is the God before whom we are ever standing. Before God and with Him we live without God. God allows Himself to be edged out of the world and on to the cross. God is weak and powerless in the world, and that is exactly the way, the only way, in which He can be with us and help us. Matthew 8:17 makes it crystal clear that it is not by his omnipotence that Christ helps us, but by his weakness and suffering. . . .
This is the decisive difference between Christianity and all religions. Man's religiosity makes him look in his distress to the power of God in the world; he uses

[2] Book Five, p. 377.

God as a *Deus ex machina*. The Bible, however, directs him to the powerlessness and suffering of God; only a suffering God can help. To this extent we may say that the process we have described by which the world came of age was an abandonment of a false conception of God, and a clearing of the decks for the God of the Bible, who conquers power and space in the world by His weakness. This must be the starting point for our 'worldly' interpretation.

DIETRICH BONHOEFFER[3]

This secular interpretation of the Gospel is not only an intellectual affair, although it requires the full commitment of the intellect. It must be incorporated in the life of the church (for is it not the Body of Christ?), and the church must suffer for it. It is not granted to everyone to take this course, and those who do take it feel that they are guided from above rather than making a spontaneous choice. It is more attractive to practice *theologia gloriae* (however false the form it may assume) than to take the dark and lonely way of the *theologia crucis*.

It is doubtful, however, whether a church which tries to have its roots in the *Corpus Christianum* will still get its message across as the *Corpus Christi*. It is true, the seed which falls into the earth and dies appears to be completely lost and there is no guarantee that it will take root, for many seeds do really die. But there is no real alternative. For it may be said with absolute certainty that the seed which remains alone will never bear fruit.

[3] *Letters and Papers from Prison*, translated from the German by Reginald H. Fuller (New York, 1962), page 163.

THREE

◻ The Role of Laity in Mission

The subtitle of the theme of this study might be "The Role of the Laity in Mission." For mission, taken as the comprehensive witness in word and deed, is "the Christian's calling"; that is the task of the whole church represented in all its members together. There is, today, a good deal of confusion about the meaning of the term "laity," which is much more ambiguous than the familiar use of the word should allow us to guess. Within the context of our theme there is neither opportunity nor a need to deal extensively with this terminological issue, but it may be helpful to distinguish at least three different approaches.

LAITY AS "LAOS"

Laity, going back to the Greek root "laos," should be interpreted as the "people of God" as it is used in the

New Testament: "laos" is identical with the church as the body of Christ. He, as the ascended Lord, through the service of apostles, prophets, evangelists, pastors, and teachers, is working "for the equipment of the saints, for the work of ministry, for building up the body of Christ until we all attain . . . to mature manhood, to the measure of the stature of the fullness of Christ" (Ephesians 4:12f.).

The laity is "the saints," or "we all," growing up to the maturity of Christ.

There is, in our time, a rediscovery of this wholeness of the church which the Reformation had emphasized in its proclamation of "the priesthood of all believers," but which also runs like dynamite, often exploding in heretic and sectarian or protest movements, throughout the course of church history. Our gratitude for this renewed insight should not, however, prevent us from making some critical remarks.

The interpretation of the laity as the church in its wholeness need not lead into a church-centered approach to the lay issue, but it certainly does not provide a guarantee against such an approach.

The question of how the inner structure of the church, conceived of as the laity, is to be understood, is still left undecided in this interpretation. One only need point to the discussions of recent decades within Roman Catholic theology. It was, for instance, not a progressive thinker like the French Jesuit père Yves M. J. Congar, but Pope Pius XII himself who already in 1946, in an address to the Holy College, declared the laity "not only to be a part of the Church, but to be themselves the Church."

The emphasis on the essential lay character of the church may work as an antidote against clericalism and hierarchical concepts, and the strong accent upon the apostolic obligation of this lay church may guard against church-directed tendencies; nevertheless, it should be realized that the result can also, apparently paradoxically, be in reverse: a lay intensification of church-centered (and for its ministry "equipped by" the hierarchy) expansionism into a de-christianized or pagan world.

A one-sided New Testament-centered interpretation of the "laos" as being identical with the church is apt to neglect the much wider and different dimensions of this concept which we meet in the rich variety of Old Testament history. Or, to put it more adequately, the Old Testament terms can only be rightly apprehended from the viewpoint of their fulfillment in the New Testament, provided this approach has been preceded by the reverse method: to hear the "overtones" of the New Testament concept as echoing against the walls of Old Testament history. Let us mention three rather arbitrarily chosen examples:

a. *Genesis 11:6:* "They are one people," says the Lord, referring to "the whole earth," still having one language, which is building the tower of Babel. The Hebrew term, being used here, is the word *am* which in general, in the Old Testament, is the *terminus technicus* for the chosen people, Israel. But here it comprehends the original unity of the whole of mankind.

b. *Genesis 12:2:* Abraham is called upon to be made into "a great nation," all the "families of the earth" being expected to bless themselves by him. The Hebrew word for "nation," which we find here is the singular (*goy*) of that term which in the Old Testament denotes, in the plural form, the "nations," that is the "gentiles" (*goyim*).

c. *I Samuel 17:46f.:* The Philistine giant Goliath is challenged by David in the following words: "This day the Lord will deliver you into my hand; that all the earth may know that there is a God in Israel, and that all this assembly may know that the Lord saves not with sword and spear." The word which is used here for "assembly" is the well-known Hebrew term "Kahal," translated in the Septuagint as *ekklesia* and is the Hebrew root of the New Testament term for church, *ekklesia*. But there is a remarkable "overtone" in the use of the term in this pericope: first, the strict analogy (of a typically Hebrew *parallelismus membrorum* of which the Psalms contain so many examples) between "all the earth" and "all this assembly"; second, the obvious distinction between the people of Israel on one hand and "all this assembly" on the other hand; third, the noticeable constituency of this "assembly," being the gathering of "onlookers" to this duel between Goliath and David, consisting of the Philistine army on one side of this natural "stadion" and the Israelite army standing on the opposite hill. In other words, the *Kahal* or *ekklesia* addressed by David is a public gathering consisting of Jews and gentiles together.

These few hints may suffice to point both to the multidimensional structure, and to its amazingly worldly and public character, of the Old Testament terms which lie at the root of the New Testament terms for "church" (*ekklesia*) and for "people of God" (*laos theou*).

Only a comprehensive exegesis which takes these Old Testament implications of the terms "laos" and "laity" in full seriousness can prevent us from a one-sided church-centered laity concept. Any isolated or one-sided New Testament-centered interpretation is, in my opinion, doomed to fall in this trap.

NINETEENTH-CENTURY LAY MOVEMENT TRADITION

A second approach stems from the lay movement tradition which is pithily summed up by John Mott's *Liberating the Lay Forces of Christianity*. Mott himself was the nearly classical representative of this type of Christian laity, and the immense contribution of this inspiring tradition to the mainstream of the modern missionary movements is still discernible in contemporary world missions assemblies.

This approach, however, should be put to the test by some critical questions and remarks.

There are various aspects of this nineteenth-century

lay movement tradition which are, implicitly, related to the above-mentioned "public" and "worldly" character of the Old Testament "laity" concept. But this relationship, in general, has hardly been devoted to serious study and thinking. These "Federations" and "Associations," and a number of missionary "movements" included, have often been borne by a rather individualistic concept of Christian faith and Christian life which launched its criticism against the immobile and massive structure of the official churches, without basing itself on a deeper understanding of the biblical—particularly Old Testament—concept of God's elected people. Therefore these movements have functioned as para- or shadow-churches rather than correctives to the church-centered concept itself.

There is in this lay movement tradition a good deal of sound reaction and, it might even be added, sound resentment against the tyranny of professional theologians, clergymen, and pastors in traditional church life. Nevertheless, it may be wondered whether this opposition is in itself sufficiently deeply anchored to withstand the enormous suction of the forces against which it is directed. In the same year that saw the publication of John Mott's book *Liberating the Lay Forces of Christianity,* the well-known *Laymen's Report* was being published. This report resulted from a trip to a number of mission posts abroad, made by a group of laymen who were leaders in the American missionary movement; it launched a devastating criticism upon the methods and activities of Christian missions overseas. But in the background of this criticism, for all the extremely healthy remarks and proposals which it contained, there was a hidden theology of mission and of the relationship between revelation and non-Christian religions which had less to do with laity or laymen than with certain theological ideas and ideals. Mott, an outspoken layman himself, asked Hendrik Kraemer to prepare a counter-attack, which he did launch indeed in his well-known book *The Christian Message in a Non-Christian World,* written in preparation of the Third World Missions Conference at Tambaram, 1938. Kraemer, though a "layman" himself like Mott and the authors of the *Laymen's Report,* recognized the basically theological presuppositions of this lay discussion: his book was, therefore, not only a specimen of profound theological thinking, but it made a grateful though critical use of the theological renewal which had been introduced by the most influential theologian of our century, Karl Barth.

What I mean to say by this reference to recent history of the missionary movement is this: that a simple appeal to one's being a "layman" has not any meaning in itself. Many laymen's pretensions and many lay oppositions are from the very outset paralyzed by an analogous frustration which doomed the rebellion of the Greek gods against the supreme power of the "Moira" (Fate) to failure. No layman who wants to say something about Christian faith, church, clergy, etc., can express himself without resorting to some sort of theological thinking. There is, to be sure, a desperate need both of a "theology of the laity" and of a "theology produced by and for laymen," but its value will consist in its being, in a primitive or in a more sophisticated form, sound theology in contradistinction to a good deal of sick, outdated, illusionary theology which is being administered by so many professional theologians. And if it cannot stand this test, all specimens of Christian lay thinking which we may hope for in the future will turn out to be nothing better than popular reiterations, in lay guise, of all too familiar theologies.

"WORLD COME OF AGE"

A third approach, therefore, is desperately needed to guard this rediscovery of the laity against disappointment and frustration. This approach has, to begin with, to avoid those very deviations which were hinted at in the preceding points. It has to take the Old Testament roots of the laity concept with deadly seriousness and it has to break through the magic circle of nineteenth-century lay movement tradition which is in danger of determining the layman as a shadow- or candidate-theologian (or candidate-clergyman) and the laity as an association or federation of Christian individuals.

To go further, a new approach has to make the bold step out of a nineteenth-century tradition into the realities of the second half of the twentieth century. In my preliminary remarks I anticipated this step when I referred to a chasm which has to be breached between John Mott and Dietrich Bonhoeffer. Though the first one was a "layman" while the second was a professional "theologian," it may be wondered whether it was not Bonhoeffer who has immensely helped us in discovering a new track.

The amazing point in Bonhoeffer's martyr's death is precisely its public character. Though in the preceding years, he was one of the leaders of the German confessing church in its opposition against National Socialism, it was not this which brought him to the gallows. No, it was his active participation in the conspiracy against Hitler, ending in the abortive assault on his life on July 20, 1944, which resulted in Bonhoeffer's final execution. He died, not as a church leader, in defense of his church, nor as a theologian who stood for his doctrine and profession, but as a "layman" who committed the supreme public crime: high treason. His act bore a political character, bearing all the familiar characteristics of open rebellion, and, had the assault succeeded, he would have been co-responsible for the formation of a new government to meet the task of ending a lost war and of recognizing the necessity of capitulation.

In other words, Bonhoeffer's action was in the line of Old Testament prophecy which was deeply concerned with the public order and which fought in favor of the restoration of justice and peace for the whole nation. There was in the history of German Christendom a fatal development of a Christian "Holy German Nation" idolatry, supported by a long tradition of Christian throne-and-altar ideology which reached its climax in the paganized pseudo-prophecy of the Third Reich mythology. This mythology had to be exposed by a radical theology—which Karl Barth was called upon to conceive—linked up with a tenacious confession of the church—inspired by Niemöller—but both lines should not have been complete without this third line of action: public resistance in a political rebellion.

There were in the July 20th conspiracy certainly a number of politicians, aristocrats, military leaders, who were deadly serious about their decision to murder Adolf Hitler but nevertheless had very vague, confused and rather old-fashioned ideas about the political and social order which would have to be built upon the ruins of Nazi Germany. They were rebels but, in the deeper sense, not prophets, both for lack of insight into the real causes of Germany's disease and for lack of vision into the fundamental renewal which would be needed. Had their conspiracy succeeded, there might have been a fair chance of political restoration according to old-fashioned concepts. It is the unique merit of Bonhoeffer that, while motivated by truly prophetic inspiration, at the same time he stood with both feet on the ground of the twentieth century, ploughed up by the upheavals of two world wars. He was a real "layman," not only from the viewpoint of his political action, but also as a seer of the "world come of age." His prophecy was really relevant for our technocratic era. His remarks, laid down in his prison letters, are, to be sure, fragmentary and here and there a little enigmatic. They are, nevertheless, for this very reason splendid specimens of "lay theology," which means they cannot be construed as a "system"; they are arbitrary thoughts produced under high pressure of all too worldly con-

cerns, cut off from any official Christian ministry within
a regular ecclesiastical order, lacking any authoritative
pretensions. We should not give way to the temptation
to develop Bonhoeffer's *pensées* into a system, but we
are certainly called upon to follow the track which he has
forged. For my part, I am inclined to think along the
following lines:

"Laity" in our time has to make a profound study
of the "public" action and thinking of Old Testament
prophecy, addressing the whole nation, vicariously acting on its behalf and willing to bear suffering and
hatred in reward for the judging Word which is being
proclaimed.

"Laity" should be conceived in the comprehensive
meaning which is revealed by the Old Testament concepts which lie at its root.

The meaning and function of the "laity" in our
technocratic era can only be discovered in the course,
and as a result, of a long-term, inter-disciplinary teamwork in which professional theology is willing without
reserve to cooperate with all those scientific and technical disciplines which determine the face of modern
civilization. We have to conceive of a new *universitas
scientiarum,* a new scientific universe, and this is exactly
opposite to the idea of the university conceived of in the
Christian Middle Ages. Instead of pretending to function as the queen of sciences, present-day theology
should be ready to become the humble servant of modern
sciences and technology. What this concretely means
nobody still knows, for this insight cannot be deduced
from the metaphysical presuppositions and theses of

traditional theology; it has to be experimentally discovered, step by step, in persevering teamwork together with other sciences—not in a speculative way,
but in a continuous encounter between hypothetical
concepts and experimental verification, between fantasy
and research, between metaphysical deductions and the
exact method of modern physics. The role of theology
will, to say the least of it, be radically different from
the role it has played in the past, but there is no alternative. The alternative would be that theology and professional theologians would rapidly lose any other function in the modern world than that of a superfluous
edification and satisfaction of religious needs.

The distinction between "laity" and "theologians,"
or "clergy," should be understood in a different way
than it is normally conceived of. The crucial point is
not what kind of profession one has, but with what
type of theology (hidden or open, conscious or unconscious) one approaches the realities of man and world
in a technocratic era. The true "laity" is not a host of
"non-theologians," but it is the group which is ready to
face the challenge of a "non-theo-logy," of an apperception of God, man, and world which starts from the
acknowledgment that the notion "God," as we have
been able to conceive of this throughout the course of
church history up to the present time, is in a rapid
process of losing its meaning. This "non-theo-logy" is
different from any "a-theistic" philosophy, for it only
starts from the assumption that the traditional ways of
approaching the theological issues are closed and that
we are compelled to open new tracks. One of the tasks

and opportunities which face us during this open adventure is certainly the dialogue with modern atheism
in its pluriform manifestations; but this dialogue will
only be part of a much more fundamental issue: the
dialogue with the scientific and technological foundations of our era.

It would, however, be hazardous to assume that this
dialogue can and should only take place on a highly
scientific level. One of the most far-reaching revolutions
of our time is the insight, forced upon us by the inven-
tion of the atomic bomb, that a separation between
"logos" and "ethos" definitely belongs to the past. There
is no longer any real possibility for scientists and technologians to escape responsibility for the revolutionizing
consequences of their inventions with their explosive
effects on the political, social, economic, and cultural
fields. In this respect also there is a need for rethinking the role of the Christian laity. This could be
aptly summed up as readiness to face the full implications of the integration between theory and practice,
logos and ethos, science (whether abstract philosophy,
physics, or theology) and politics.

The preceding remarks make it perfectly clear that
the role of the "Christian laity" can no longer be
separated from the more general questions of mankind's
answer to the suicidal dangers which we are facing
today. Only integrated cooperation among *all* sciences
will be able to meet this challenge and only standing
teamwork between "Christians" and "non-Christians"
will be adequate. This does not mean that the distinction
between faith and unbelief, between being a Christian

and not being a Christian, will be effaced. To the contrary: it is just in the course of this enduring teamwork and only in this contact that the real, the relevant distinction will become evident. It is just by this way, and only in this indissoluble cooperation, that the real dialogue about the fundamental issues of God's revelation in Christ to a lost world will develop.

In the course of this process there will, to be sure, develop a "Christian laity," which cuts across the familiar distinction between "clergy" and "layman," for this enduring teamwork will require a new series of ministries. When theology will be reborn and become relevant again for modern science and technology, there will rise a new type of scientist who will be anxious to plunge into the mysteries and perspectives of this enigmatic, ungraspable, and yet unescapable science; and it will, conversely, become normal for a theologian to combine his specialization with a profound knowledge of one of the exact sciences or with some special technological discipline.

This "Christian laity" will also embrace "Christians" and "non-Christians" alike, for the crucial test will not be whether one answers to the familiar labels but to what degree one is willing and is capable to partake in this cooperative adventure of twentieth-century prophecy.

In the course of modern history the "nation" concept, which is a cornerstone of the building of western democracy, has developed in intimate relationship to that extent of democratic consciousness which was being fostered within the Christian churches. Democracy, in order to stand the trial of modern technocratic society, will have to pass through fundamental changes. The role of the "Christian laity" in this process of renewal will be dependent upon its capacity to give a new vision to the whole nation and to the international commonwealth of everyman's opportunity and duty really to participate in the evolution of a responsible society.

All this, apparently, in first instance applies to the task of the laity at home. Truly it is there at the "home base" that the capacity of the laity to fulfill a ministry "overseas" is being decided. The missioners' contribution "overseas" will be exactly to help fellows in other continents to answer the analogous questions and to meet the same challenges which we have to answer and to meet "at home."

FOUR

▣ Theocracy, Ontocracy, Technocracy

THE RISE OF THE WEST
AND ITS GLOBAL EXPANSION

Prophecy, as we can learn from the Old Testament prophets, is the theocratic ministry par excellence: it is not concerned with anything lesser than the reign of the Lord ("theo-cracy"). The type of culture and society in which the Old Testament prophets bore their witness was qualitatively different from our present-day society which I have characterized as "technocratic." It is a historical fact that this type of modern "technocratic society" has originated in the West, more particularly in western Europe—the industrial revolution which started its career in Great Britain being the decisive breakthrough of a new evolution of human society. It

83

was the United States which eagerly took over the industrial banner and which intensified and accelerated this unique development. It was the expansion of the West which distributed this new technological revolution all over the world or—as we have grown familiar to say—to the "East," which is becoming increasingly "westernized."

For the missionary movement of today it may be interesting to get an insight into this cultural and social evolution, for the simple reason that this belongs to the "scheme of this world" which it has pleased God to address with the good news of the Gospel. There are a number of fascinating general theories about this evolution: Arnold Toynbee's *A Study of History* has acquired world-wide influence among our generation; the work of the American historian William McNeill, entitled *The Rise of the West,* is a more recent specimen. For all the great differences regarding approach and viewpoint between these two historians, they have at least three important characteristics in common.

1. Both have attempted to design a general theory of the evolution of cultures throughout the course of world history: Toynbee's theory is of a succession of twenty-one "societies," McNeill's idea is of a changing balance within the Eurasian *ecumene* of four major civilizations.

2. Both theories culminate in the rise of western civilization which is described on one hand as the application of a general historical law of evolution; on the other hand, the unprecedented character of the modern

West is implicitly acknowledged—its global dispersion and (in Toynbee's study) the "open" trend of its future (as contrasted with the already closed evolution of all other living societies).

3. Neither historian has ascribed to Israel's history and society a particular, let alone unique, significance.

It seems doubtful, to say the least, whether an approach to world historic evolution that fails to do justice to the peculiar position and quality of biblical history and to the impact of the biblical view upon history does not lack the most essential characteristics. For the benefit of Christian mission we can learn an immense lot from these historians' views. Nevertheless, we must put them to the same crucial test which we ourselves have to stand. It is the *raison d'être* of Christian mission to witness to the "fullness of time" which has come in Jesus the Messiah of Israel and which we are still looking forward to in the final consummation of history. The unique character of Israel's history is a decisive factor in this consummation.

Thus we must develop a theory of history that takes into account all that is implied in the biblical view. How we define our theory of history is of direct relevance to the theme of prophecy in a technocratic era. We must take into consideration the following:

An approach which acknowledges the radical breach which in Israel's history has been made by the prophets upon the total pattern of ancient religion and society is *a priori* open-minded toward the possible relationship that may be discernible between this encroachment and the other radical impact upon this total pattern that has been produced by the technocratic development of modern society.

An approach which from the very outset considers human history in the light of the unique fact of God's revelation is *a priori* inclined to recognize unique historical events and developments.

An approach that is true to the horizons that are opened up in the eschatological perspectives of the Bible is anxious to penetrate into the deeper meaning of the revolutionary mutations of human existence which we are facing in the rise of a universally expanding technocratic society.

A NEW APPROACH

An approach of this kind means, to be sure, a far cry from our common way of interpreting modern history and of interpreting biblical history. Its implications can be defined as follows. The overarching pattern in the great cultural and religious traditions of the ancient Near East and of the Asian continent is the common rule of throne-and-altar. In the course of western Christian history the first pillar of this dual foundation has been gravely undermined by the rise of democracy; the evolution of technocracy has dealt heavy blows to the second pillar. Whereas the democratic revolution affects the societal structure that found its culminating point in the royal palace, the technocratic revolution, rooted in modern science, means a deathblow to that apperception of the universe of which the Temple has always and everywhere been the supreme symbolism.

There is, to be sure, no direct link between the development of western democracy and biblical concepts of the people's covenant with the Lord, but it is hard to deny that this biblical inspiration, in former centuries, has been of important and sometimes decisive influence. To the extent, however, that the concept of western democracy lost its religious foundation and turned into the proclamation of the people's sovereignty, this link became increasingly loosened.

Whereas, regarding democracy, there is already an important distance, we have apparently to face an unbridgeable gap between modern technocracy and the biblical apperception of God, man, and universe. Without attempting to deny the existence of this gap or to belittle its size, we should, however, make some important distinctions:

a. This gap is not only related to biblical tradition but to the whole religious tradition of mankind.
b. There is also a gap, by no means less wide and deep, between the biblical apperception of creation and the religious ideas about the universe which dominated the civilizations of the ancient Near East and of the Asian continent. This opposition is summed up in the prophetic criticism upon the Temple, culminating in Jesus' final judgment, proclaimed by Paul's witness of the man-made character of all temples.

There are, thus, not two, but three different apperceptions which have to be distinguished:

1. Theocracy (the prophetic witness to the Lord's reign).
2. Ontocracy (the general pattern of throne-and-altar).
3. Technocracy (the modern apperception of a man-made society and a man-made universe).

There is, as it were, a triangular relationship and mutual contradistinction between these three viewpoints:

How one views these relationships is mainly dependent upon the priority given to a certain viewpoint. Our familiar approach is to stress the opposition of our technocratic civilization over against pre-industrial civilizations. Looking from this point of view, one sees the pattern of religious civilizations in a common perspective with the biblical type of culture. There is, indeed, a good deal of agreement between both patterns. Not only has the cultural evolution in the ancient Near East and in the Hellenistic world formed the general background of Old and New Testament concepts, but what is more important, this also pertains, to a certain extent, to the religious message of the Bible. In the Old Testament the unique name of *Jahweh* is closely linked up with the general divine title *elohim*, whereas in the New Testament both the terms *Kurios* and *theos*, being the unique and the more general titles of the God and Father of Jesus Christ or of Jesus himself, are closely associated with familiar notions of pagan Greek religion.

When we start, however, from one of the other two viewpoints, the scene changes. From the angle of theocracy, there is not only a contrast with modern technocracy, but biblical theocracy is in irreconcilable enmity against the ontocratic foundation of the surrounding cultures. Under the surface of a common religious heritage and terminology, there runs an irreparable breach, separating general religious apperceptions from the unique witness to the Lord.

Looking from the angle of the ontocratic pattern, we make the somewhat surprising discovery that "theocracy" and "technocracy" can be drawn into a common perspective, namely, as the two radical opposites of ontocracy. Recapitulating, we find the following three combinations:

1. The apperception of the *Corpus Christianum* period which reconciled or confused "theocracy" and "ontocracy" with each other. This fusion was, apparently, supported by the fact that in the Bible itself the prophetic message is dressed in the garb of a general religious terminology.

2. We find the phenomena of "renascent religions" in non-western countries and, perhaps, of a "religious boom" in the United States. These phenomena seem to point to the latent potentialities of "ontocratic" traditions to become revivified by the stimuli of the technocratic impact. Conversely, the development of Chinese Communism may lead into attempts to graft a technocratic ideology upon an ontocratic (Confucianist) tradition.

3. The third combination has, as yet, been hardly

explored. The idea of observing "theocracy" and "tech-nocracy" as allies is new and, for many of us, repulsive. It has, indeed, to overcome two serious barriers: the still deeply ingrained heritage of the *Corpus Christianum* tradition and, more fundamental, the "ontocratic" con-text of Old and New Testament. To rethink the church's witness and attitude face to face with the un-precedented possibilities and challenges of this common perspective is the very task which is implicit in our theme "prophecy in a technocratic era."

CONSEQUENCES FOR OUR MISSION

The universal impact of the technocratic era upon the ontocratic structures forces us to confront the bibli-cal contrast between theocracy and ontocracy with the present-day clash between technocracy and ontocracy. For our witness to the biblical message, this means that we have to attempt to translate this message in such terms that its promise amid the decay and fall of onto-cratic ideas and structures can be heard and understood.

Since mankind today finds itself in a great variety of situations, varying from stone-age social structure and mental attitudes to those of the second industrial revo-lution, and from tribal religion to modern atheism or nihilism, only a great variety of missionary approaches and ways of presenting the Gospel can meet so many different levels of existence and of understanding. There is, however, one guiding principle which should direct any approach; namely, the need of preparing our generation for an adequate response to the impact of technocratic society. Points of contact with non-Christian religious traditions may be a useful and necessary bridge to allow the biblical message to penetrate into a foreign civilization. The decisive and essential points of contact of today are, however, on those crossroads where the technocratic impact encroaches upon age-old religious heritage.

Just as the prophets and apostles of Old and New Testament could not strip from their messages the cultural and religious notions of their time and environment, neither can the missionary movement of today do without the modes of expression of our century. There is, however, an important difference. Whereas the biblical messengers communicated with a public which shared with them a common cultural and social level, the modern missionary movement makes full use of a variety of instruments (printing press, colleges, hospitals and drugs, machines for rural development and airplanes for traveling, etc.) which belong to the more advanced phases of technological and scientific development. These instruments cannot be dealt with as negligible means to reach the missionary goal, for they are in many cases of a much further reaching and enduring influence than the spoken message itself; they determine in an often decisive manner the way in which the message is being heard or misunderstood. And, last but not least, they are being used in missionary action, because they are considered the most adequate instruments for serving our fellowman in a technocratic age.

HERESIES

It belongs to the historical character of mission that the Gospel can never be put under "pure" culture. The Gospel is not an idea or a theory, but, being the promise of the coming re-creation, it aims at drawing the world into the movement toward that ultimate goal. In the course of that process not only is the Gospel influencing and changing the world, but it is being changed itself.

Of the most delusory and dangerous metamorphoses which the Gospel may pass through, the Bible gives us impressive examples. In the Old Testament we read that the Israelites "built the high places of Ba'al in the valley of the son of Hinnom, to offer up their sons and daughters to Molech" (Jer. 32:35). The name *Molech* is an ignominious term, given by the prophets in order to stigmatize this idolatry which was not devoted to some kind of pagan god, but to the *melech,* the Lord of Israel. The prophets stigmatized this by changing the vowels of the word *melech* into the vowels of the Hebrew word for "ignominy," or "scandal," namely *bosheth,* so that the word *melech* was turned into the word *molech.*

In the New Testament we read that "even Satan disguises himself as an angel of light" (2 Cor. 11:14). The confession of Christ can become the confession of the anti-Christ, under Christ's name. Peter's confession near Caesarea Philippi "You are the Christ, the Son of the Living God" is revealed to him by the Father who is in heaven, but the next moment the same Peter is being revealed as Satan: "You are a hindrance to me;

for you are not on the side of God, but of men" (Matt. 16:13–23). It is the very temptation which assaulted Jesus in the desert: Christ himself can become anti-Christ, under Christ's name and with his face and dress. It is the old temptation of the chosen people which wanted "a King to govern us like all nations" (1 Samuel 8:5). From the very outset of its career through the world of the gentiles, the Gospel has not only faced the alternatives of conversion or aversion, but it has been astoundingly prolific in producing a type of by-product which bears the familiar trade-mark. Apart from this, there is also a third possibility: that this bastard does not value bearing the name of the father, but, on the contrary, starts a competing firm with a new brand which is, of course, "better" than the old one.

To sum up, evangelization faces the following results:

a. conversion
b. some bastard type of "Christendom" or "Church"
c. some kind of antagonist.

If these three lines of development were clearly distinguishable, there might not be a serious problem. But, in fact, these lines are intersecting and intermingling and, what enhances the problem, even where they are purely following their own direction, it is not easy to discern the genuine character of each line: our familiar labels are, more often than not, misleading. There is no pure "conversion" which has not, at least, the potentiality of developing typical "bastard" qualities, or even turning into a counter-faith or counter-church.

There is no form of Christianity and no type of church, no matter how far it has "deviated," which has lost all contact with the original message; and, conversely, no bulwark of Christian faith is safe from the danger that its soldiers may start a rebellion and direct their weapons against their own army. With respect to the third line, the same remarks can be made. The driving force behind antagonist ideas and movements is their paradoxical relationship to the original appeal to conversion which they repeat in another form and with new words. And to the extent that they are stigmatized by the "true church" and the "genuine Christendom" as heresy, they present their public prosecutors with a mirror in which they can look at their own "heretical" face.

For the sake of Mission this insight is of constitutional significance. We the Christian church who are going "overseas" in order to proclaim the good message of conversion and salvation are not only unavoidably going to produce "heresies," but we enter upon a world which is already full of "heresies" which have been produced in a more remote or a recent past, and of these "heresies" we are, in all probability, the most splendid and most carefully disguised specimen ourselves. Proverbs like "the pot calls the kettle black" and "ill-doers are ill-deemers" may give evidence of all too popular psychology. They may also refer to the profound biblical judgment, that "the measure you give will be the measure you get" (Matt. 7:2). Nobody is able to see his own face but in a mirror, and it is for this very reason that we are astonishingly clairvoyant in ascribing our own features to our rivals.

IMMUNIZATION

A classical example of this historical process is the rise of Islam, a phenomenon which is at the same time:

a. a counter-church
b. a counter-Christendom
c. a counter-civilization.

In all these respects, Islam discloses the specific qualities of an "immunization" process resulting in a product which is safeguarded against precisely those diseases which it has, just a little, passed through by itself. To the church, Islam offers that deep-rooted and inconquerable resistance which is an essential feature of "heretical" consciousness, overtrumping the church by its own cards. As a counter-Christendom it is the incarnation of just those self-righteous pretensions which form the backbone of Christendom. And as a counter-civilization, Islam has started its career as the predetermined competitor of a Hellenized Christendom and a western Christian course of development. An extraordinarily important characteristic of Islam is that it does not attempt to distinguish these three viewpoints from each other. For this very reason, our Christian mission can learn in the encounter with Islam so many immensely useful lessons in self-knowledge and self-criticism. Facing this counter-church we have to ask ourselves whether our missionary action in the Islamic world has not been throughout the centuries until today frustrated not only by the historical law of immunization which accompanies the history of evangelization, but by the fact that we ourselves, the Christian church, have been brought forth as a result of such a process. Have we not escaped from radically recognizing this unpleasant truth by our theological solution which manages to distinguish between "faith" and "civilization," between "church" and "world," between the "Gospel" and "society"? Is not Islam much more realistic and true to the facts when it denies the possibility of making these pure distinctions and when it deals with church, Christendom, and Christian civilization as simply one indissoluble complex?

This question should also be reversed. When we are convinced that, nevertheless, in this confused and complex whole in which church, Christendom, and Christian civilization are intermingled, the Lord is actively dealing with His people and fulfilling His purposes, why should we exclude this anti-church, anti-Christendom and anti-civilization from this supposition? This is not a rhetorical or theoretical question, nor a theological issue, but it is directly relevant in regard to the present situation which the Christian church is facing within its own society. Western Christian civilization has reached an unprecedented phase of history in which the very pillars of the "ontocratic" structure which, in Christian forms, has determined the *Corpus Christianum* period of western history, are going to pieces. This does not only affect the Christian church, but the "anti-church" of Islam is challenged in the same manner by this development. Throughout the centuries the encounter between Christianity and Islam has been paralyzed by the fact that two antagonists were raising analogous but mutually contradicting claims, both of them being safely protected behind the walls of their respective civilizations. The onrush of technocratic society is in process of ruining these walls and of challenging these claims. Both Christianity and Islam are entering upon an era in which they have to face unprecedented questions for which there are no traditional answers, and in which they have to meet challenges for which the bulwarks of the past do not offer sufficient protection.

There is, to be sure, the phenomenon of what is commonly called "the renascence of religions." This phenomenon does not only refer to Islam but to the great religious traditions of Asia as well. To the extent that Christian missions are affected, we may be inclined to explain this phenomenon as a new example of the law of "immunization," this time being the revival of anti-Christian consciousness by the impact of modern western Christian civilization which has penetrated into the body of the non-western societies. We should, however, see to it, that we do not meet this religious renascence in the same style as, in the past, the "Christian world" has conceived of the encounter with the Islamic world. For, whatever the threat these renascent religions may offer to a *Corpus Christianum* structure of Christianity, under the surface of this enhanced self-consciousness they stand as puzzled and as helpless as Christianity itself. And it is precisely in this common exposure to unanswered questions and unprecedented dangers and opportunities, that there are opening up new fields of encounter between Christians and non-Christians all over the world.

THE ENCOUNTER WITH COMMUNISM

This historical law of the rise of heresies, of which the career of Islam is the genuinely classical example, finds in modern times an analogous culminating point in the career of communism. It is not exaggerated to state that the encounter with communism is the most comprehensive issue which confronts the church in our century. Here we face a challenge in which the Christian mission is being put to the test *in toto* and whereby our actual credentials are being questioned. It is upon this battlefield that our capacity of being really prophetic in a technocratic era is exposed to the light.

The western Christian world, and the United States in particular, apparently have a number of splendid possibilities at their disposal to escape a real encounter or to enter upon this arena from the wrong side and with inadequate weapons:

   a. The Christian church has, in the nineteenth century, in general failed to meet the fundamental questions which were put to it by Karl Marx and by the rise of the socialist and communist movement. For the U.S.A. there was a great geographical distance in addition.
   b. The atheist materialism of communist philosophy has a rather old-fashioned make-up, being

the heritage of nineteenth-century scientific materialism.

c. Marx' prophecy of a communist revolution in the capitalist West has been disavowed by the facts and, apart from France and Italy, the communist parties in western countries are of negligible political importance.

d. Communism appears only to have serious attraction in underdeveloped countries, so that efficient aid to these countries seems to be in the future the adequate answer of the western, highly developed world to this challenge.

e. In communist countries there is no freedom for the Christian church and all missionary activity is radically suppressed. Western churches are, therefore, cut off from contact with the communist world.

f. The communist victory in China means a scandal and an obsession particularly for American churches and missions which have been so suddenly cut off from a mission field which had been the apple of their eye and to which they had devoted their dearest forces and expectations.

g. In the short run there seems to be no other possibility than political and military vigilance abroad and defense against communist penetration at home. In the long run, there may be a chance of decay and increasing incoherence of the communist bloc, of doctrinal and social

evolution of communist countries into a miti-
gated "bourgeois" direction and of winning the
underdeveloped world by the attractive perspectives of the "free world."

This in broad outline being the situation, there
seems, indeed, for the Christian church hardly to exist
any reason or incentive to start a real dialogue with communism and to take its spiritual challenge with profound
seriousness.

On each of the above-mentioned points a critical
comment may, nevertheless, be made:

a. The missed opportunity of the nineteenth century forces the Christian church to make up for
a hundred years of negligence. The class struggle within nineteenth-century western society
was a minor problem as compared with the
world-wide challenge which communism is of-
fering today.

b. Communist materialism is, far from being an
outdated philosophy, a double heritage of modern western civilization. As historical materialism it designs a comprehensive explanation of
the meaning of world history, and as dialectical
materialism it attempts to summarize all scientific knowledge about the structure of the universe. Its atheism is a protest against the failure
of Christian theology to answer the questions
of our technocratic age and a consequence of
that atheistic humanism which lay in the background of the rise of western bourgeoisie and
of modern science and technology.

c. Karl Marx has, from the very outset, put his analysis of the capitalist system within a much wider context of a worldwide struggle between industrialized and pre-industrial societies. Over against his wrong prognosis of western development stands his farseeing prediction of the chances in Russia and upon the Asian continent.

d. The fact that communism appears to be attractive for underdeveloped countries may be an indication that its social system and its concepts are more adequate precisely for these situations. In this case, the western world will have to learn a good deal from the communist approach.

e. The attitude of communist governments in relation to the Christian church is decisively determined by a deep-rooted resentment of the European proletariat in the nineteenth century against the Christian bourgeoisie and by the conviction that the church cannot be otherwise than a handmaid of the western Christian, capitalist world. This attitude can, in the future, only be changed, when the Christian churches in communist countries and the western churches are capable of a different encounter with communism than the anti-communist fear and hatred of nineteenth-century bourgeoisie.

f. Chinese communism, instead of being felt as a scandal and an obsession, should be approached by Christian missions as the great historical opportunity and challenge to rethink radically the missionary obligation for our time.

g. A merely negative long-term perspective gives evidence of a sterile mentality and a lack of vision which can never hope to win the adherence of developing countries which more urgently than material aid are in need of an approach which opens up new tracks towards a better future. The crucial issue is not whether in the long run communism will fail, but whether we have a real alternative.

Communism is the ideology and the movement that most comprehensively confronts us with our theme "prophecy in a technocratic era":

1. It pretends to know the meaning of history, as this was revealed by its prophet, Karl Marx: discerning the signs of the time, forecasting judgment and catastrophe to the existing society, appealing to conversion, prophesying the coming era of abiding justice and peace.

2. It has a burning sense of mission, seeing the whole world as ripening for the coming harvest of the new man and the new society. Into this harvest its messengers and apostles are being sent out.

3. It is the logical conclusion of the agnosticism and actual atheism of modern science and technology, the latent background and the practical consequences of which it has summarized in a scandalous, doctrinal formula. In this respect, it is to be considered as the latest and most consistent phase of an ongoing process of secularization.

4. The communist revolution in Russia and, a generation later, in China can be understood as the transmutations of the French revolution, applied to a full-fledged ontocratic society. As an atheist revolution against the age-old structure of throne-and-altar, it confronts mankind with the most painful questions concerning the meaning of theocracy in a technocratic era.

5. It is the most important heresy of the twentieth century: counter-church, counter-Christendom, and counter-civilization at once.

Therefore, the answer to communism cannot be given by the Christian church alone, but only by an approach which sees both Christianity and communism in the context of this total perspective of western Christian history and of the future of mankind in a technocratic era.

F I V E

⊡ Development and Revolution

EVANGELISM AND DEVELOPMENT

Our theme "prophecy in a technocratic era" also can be approached from the viewpoint of the most influential guiding principle of world-wide socio-economic policy in our day, the idea of development. Whereas the agrarian pattern of the neolithic era has a static character, technocracy is essentially dynamic, because it is continuously being propelled by the ongoing stream of research and inventions. In another dimension, the same refers to the prophetic approach to man and world, which is essentially dynamic and directed toward radical change and renewal.

In the term "prophecy" also a bridge is to be found between development and evangelism, for real prophecy is both a spoken message and an actual interference in the course of history. Development is the twin brother of evangelism, and mission could be defined as:

Mission = evangelism + development.

There is here a certain analogy with the dogmatic definitions:

The work of the Holy Spirit = justification
                                                  + sanctification.

The work of Christ = eschatological + historical.

In the history of Christian missions we always find, to be sure, some kind of combination between *kerygma* and *diakonia,* between Word and service. But the ultimate accent was, in general, laid upon the eschatological aspect as a witness to the unique work of Christ in preaching and healing, resulting in total conversion and total restoration. In a preceding chapter the historical character of evangelization has strongly been emphasized. In the same manner we have now to deal with the historical character of service, which is defined by the term "development." Over against the evangelistic concept of individual conversion, development refers to a process which covers a long time span. And in contrast to a traditional missionary concept of service, it refers to a collective, structural, socio-cultural process.

We cannot, therefore, deal with the idea of development as merely belonging to the diaconal aspect of mission. Just as missionary service is ultimately determined by the concept of evangelism, in the same way, conversely, the concept of development encroaches upon our ideas about the meaning of evangelism. There are three aspects of the development concept which should be pointed to:

   a. It depends on a definite view of the meaning of history as a progressive course in the direction of an ultimate goal in which the whole of history will be consummated.

   b. The modern concept of development one-sidedly refers to the technological norm. Consequently, it is based upon a definite faith in the meaning of technology.

   c. Technological development within a pre-industrial society is only possible after a definite "takeoff" has encroached upon the traditional, self-perpetuating pattern of culture. In this break it becomes evident that development is not an automatic process but that it is dependent upon a decisive attitude.

DIALECTICS OF DEVELOPMENT

The idea of development has made its career in the modern period of western Christian civilization as the outcome of a secularized view of the meaning of history ("défatalization de la Providence," as Proudhon conceived of it). In this idea of progress we find a dialectical relationship between evolution and revolution:

   a. In a pre-revolutionary period, wherein it has to struggle against the ancient regime and the status quo, the appeal to development has a revolutionary attitude. Example: the rising bourgeoisie which prepared the French revolution of 1789.

b. As soon as victory has been won and the revolution is over, the same appeal to development gets an evolutionary twist. Example: the French bourgeoisie after the French revolution.

In the Communist Manifesto Karl Marx has keenly analyzed this dialectic. The bourgeoisie (thus can his statement be summarized):

a. is by itself the product of a protracted socio-economic evolution;

b. has played an extremely revolutionary role in modern history;

c. has produced by itself the weapons and the revolutionaries which are destined to dig its grave: the proletariat.

We can, however, discover in the later development of communism a repetition of the dialectical process which Marx has applied to former phases of history. Karl Marx designed a revolutionary doctrine: of the dialectical sequence of class struggles by which in each successive period the class that has achieved its power by revolution is to be defeated by the class it had been exploiting. The essence of these successive revolutions is to be found in the socio-economic law which causes the forces of production to break through the too-narrow limitations of outdated structures of production. The meaning of this dialectical process is to be clarified by the dialectical structure of world history, in accordance with the formal method of the Hegelian philosophy of history.

In a post-revolutionary period, this Marxist revolutionary doctrine is predestined to turn into an evolutionary view of ongoing progress: a socialist phase will gradually evolve into the ultimate phase of full-fledged communism. Communist pedagogics see to it that post-revolutionary man will proceed in the direction of the all-round type of man who has been given full scope for his mental and physical gifts. Economic planning guarantees maximal unfolding of all production forces.

These diachronical dialectics are also to be found in a synchronic fashion. Examples: Marx and Engels, being themselves members of the bourgeoisie, turned the pre-revolutionary dynamics of their own class against its post-revolutionary position; Chinese communism pretends to continue the ongoing revolution, in contrast with post-revolutionary Soviet Russia, which is being accused of becoming "bourgeois."

It is the intertwinement of these diachronical and these synchronical dialectics which together, so to speak, represent warp and woof of the development process. Here the heart of the tension between developed and underdeveloped (or developing) countries is to be found. The American economist W. W. Rostow, in his well-known study *The Stages of Economic Growth*, has given an outline of development, starting with Great Britain in the last quarter of the eighteenth century and with Asian countries like China and India at the bottom.

He calls communism "a disease of the transition" and presents his own approach as "a non-communist manifesto." We should realize, however, that there is a synchronical dialectics at that, and that the present world scene is primarily determined by these synchronical conflicts and tensions. Each more advanced stage of development unavoidably puts pressure on those stages which are lagging behind, and, reversely, the later one has joined the race, so much the more energy has to be developed to catch up with those who have started earlier.

developed stages $\leftrightarrows$ underdeveloped stages

post-revolutionary evolution $\leftrightarrows$
pre-evolutionary revolution

THE FOUR FREEDOMS UPSIDE DOWN

The development problem can be aptly described by the dialectics which are inherent in the declaration of the "Four Freedoms," made in Franklin D. Roosevelt's presidential address to the Congress on January 6, 1941, in the midst of the second World War:

> In the future days, which we seek to make secure, we look forward to a world founded upon four essential human freedoms.

> The first is freedom of speech and expression—everywhere in the world. The second is freedom of every person to worship God in his own way—everywhere in the world. The third is freedom from want which, translated into world terms, means economic under-

standings which will secure to every nation a healthy peacetime life for its inhabitants—everywhere in the world. The fourth is freedom from fear which, translated into world terms, means a world-wide reduction of armaments to such a point and in such a thorough fashion that no nation will be in a position to commit an act of physical aggression against any neighbor—anywhere in the world.

There is, in this splendid declaration, a hidden problem. The declaration keeps silence about two other freedoms which have accompanied the growth of the first and second freedom, namely the freedom of the sovereign nation and the freedom of enterprise. These two neglected freedoms are increasingly interfering with the growth of the third and fourth freedoms. Furthermore, the first and second freedoms have hardly any connection with the third and fourth freedoms.

The first and second freedoms are becoming increasingly problematical:

a. by the growth of an agnostic and atheistic pattern of modern life;
b. by the rise of modern mass society;
c. by the reaction of anti-liberal philosophies and movements.

In a somewhat roughly schematic way, the four freedoms could be defined as the characteristic expressions of four centuries:

freedom of religion	17th century
freedom of speech and expression	18th century
freedom from want	19th century
freedom from fear	20th century

The United States has had the privilege of passing through the history of discovery, proclamation, and development of these freedoms in a protracted evolutionary process. Therefore it can stand on the solid foundation that to a great extent the first three freedoms have been realized at home, and proclaim these principles as a worldwide program. And, starting from this self-satisfied optimism, it can declare to the rest of mankind its willingness to contribute to the realization of the last freedom, freedom from fear.

There are, however, other countries which approach the question from a completely different viewpoint. They look at the first and second freedoms as the presuppositions which, closely connected with nationalism and free enterprise, have enabled the United States to reach a stage of affluence, that is, of economic and military power, which, far from being the condition for universal affluence and peace, is the very barrier that baffles the way to worldwide welfare and disarmament. Those countries that have not passed through the same historical evolution as the United States but as latecomers on the scene find themselves confronted with the final result of this evolution, the overwhelming power of the United States, are inclined to revert the sequence of the four freedoms and to give highest priority to freedom from fear and to universal freedom from want. And they assume that in a disarmed and affluent world, there will be room enough to guarantee the first and second freedoms.

Let us, therefore, cast a little more careful look at the third and the fourth freedoms.

THE FOURFOLD POVERTY

A German scholar of demographic science, Gün-
ther Wollny, has, in his study *Die Zukunft ist anders*
(*The Future Is Different*) described four phases of the
poverty problem:

1. In agrarian society poverty belongs to the normal
structure of society.

2. In a transitional phase of beginning industrialization this traditional phenomenon of poverty grows
into a problem. It was in this phase that Karl Marx
wrote his analysis of nineteenth-century capitalism.

3. In an industrialized society poverty has lost its
necessary function and it does not any longer need to be
a problem.

4. The underdeveloped (or developing) countries
of today are going to face a fourth and unprecedented
type of poverty, namely that the traditional, agrarian
kind of poverty has been intensified by the decrease of
death rate, resulting from the impact of highly developed countries, or, to put it in other words, from the
dangers of partial modernization. The actual world
situation is, in fact, overshadowed by the contrast between the industrialized societies which, in principle,
have overcome the poverty problem, and the developing
countries which face an immensely aggravated poverty
problem. And it is the very fact of development that is
continuously producing and increasingly intensifying
the problem.

DEVELOPMENT AND WORLD PEACE

There are analogous problems in the background of the declaration of freedom from fear. Highly developed nations, in possession of atomic weapons, will give first priority to being safe against an atomic attack launched by other developed atomic powers. Because of their need for this safeguard, their economic and technical development is moving further and further from the stage of underdeveloped countries. Freedom from fear in a world of sovereign nations is irreconcilable with universal freedom from want.

The developed atomic powers are in need of a stabilized world situation in which peace is, in fact, identical with a status quo under their supervision. The underdeveloped nations, revolutionized by the tide of rising expectations, set all their hopes on a rapidly and radically changing world order and a new distribution of power and affluence. In both respects, a post-revolutionary view is in conflict with a pre-revolutionary view. Whereas the first view is most afraid of atomic threat and of revolutionary upheavals, the second view, in contrast, is most afraid of increasing power of the affluent countries and of a world order which is stabilized by the extremely dangerous atomic power of the developed nations. Once again, freedom from fear and freedom from want are incompatible.

THE DILEMMA OF DEVELOPMENT AID

It may have become evident that "development" is an extremely explosive process, full of inner contradictions and paradoxes. It is no wonder that the idea of development aid is beset with analogous contradictions.

a. There is the general contradiction of aid, given by developed countries which are seeking by themselves the support of underdeveloped countries in order to tip the balance of power in a divided world. Aid, given in such a situation, will unavoidably imply military aid, which is the very negation of development aid. The hand, extended to friends, is covered with an iron glove.

b. The ongoing increase in economic and technical power of the aiding countries is continuously widening the chasm which they try to bridge by giving their assistance to underdeveloped countries.

c. The western affluent countries, in fear of revolutions which result from this increasing chasm, are tempted to direct their aid precisely to those governments and circles which defend the status quo of hopeless underdevelopment.

d. "Aid" has an ethical flavor, not only to the extent that it is being given by "our free world," but for the simple reason that it is "aid." This aid ethics tends to disguise the glaring dilemmas of development aid and is, unless a radical self-criticism and unremittent analysis succeeds in breaking through, doomed to degenerate into a smug pharisaism.

THE DILEMMA OF CHRISTIAN AID

Against this background the dilemma of Christian development aid becomes obvious. We can learn a good deal from the way the church has, in the nineteenth century, tried to answer the problem of proletarian misery and poverty in the industrializing societies of western Europe. In the same year, 1848, when Marx and Engels published the *Communist Manifesto*, a German Christian, Johann Heinrich Wichern, proclaimed the program of the "Innere Mission" which has developed a rich variety of Christian diaconal initiatives. This program was, to a certain extent, an extemporized answer to the *Communist Manifesto*. The decisive contrast between the approach of Wichern and of Marx consisted in the fact that the first one, trying to meet the needs of the rising tide of industrialization, did not encroach upon the socio-economic and political structures, but on the contrary, indirectly contributed to their preservation. Therefore his impressive diaconal program had a tragic analogy with the attitude of a shipping trade board which provides its definitely unseaworthy ships with life buoys, lifeboats, life belts, and lifelines. The message of Marx was based on the proof that the ship was totally unseaworthy and on the assertion that the shipping trade board was not willing nor able to repair it or to replace it with a new one. Consequently he summoned the crew to strike and mutiny and to found a new shipping trade by themselves. The vehemently anti-Christian character of his message was partly due to his experience and conviction that it was exactly the magic power of Christian piety that it blinded the insight and paralyzed the capacities which were needed for radical measures.

In a roughly schematic outline the contrast can be summed up in the sketch on page 117.

The social question of the second half of the twentieth century is, to a certain extent, a worldwide expansion of the social question which Wichern and Marx were facing in the middle of the nineteenth century. There are, to be sure, some important differences which make for an immense aggravation of the problem:

 a. The rapid progress of industrialization in western countries has led to the rise of the welfare state which, in principle, is on the way to overcoming the poverty problem. The same process, however, has been accompanied by or has led to the unprecedented phenomenon of two world wars and to the threat of atomic war.

 b. Whereas the industrialized nations of the West have, in principle, overcome class struggle, their affluence has not contributed to worldwide progress but is in process of widening the gap with the underdeveloped nations.

 c. Whereas there was and still is, within the context of the national state, essentially a possibility for a successful national "war on poverty," there does not exist even a shadow of an analo-

Wichern	Socio-political structure	Marx
"Innere Mission"	Christian bourgeoisie	Communist Manifesto
restoration of the Christian people	*Corpus Christianum*	proclamation of atheist society
ideal of the Christian nation	throne-and-altar	atheist revolution
national program	nationalism	international class-struggle
pre-industrial diaconate	first phase of industrialism	movement of industrial proletariat
individual salvation, micro-approach	maintenance of status quo and existing macro-structure	collective salvation by radical, macro-structural renewal
evolutionary pedagogics	enlightened self-consciousness	revolutionary appeal
assistance to helpless poor	structural misery	self-liberation of labor class
building a bridge	class conflict	promise of classless society
preaching of love and peace	structural violence	structural renewal by violence
piecemeal diagnoses	industrialization	socio-economic analysis

gous international world order to attack the same problem on a worldwide scale.

d. The character of the poverty problem on a worldwide scale, today, is different from and much more serious than the analogous problem was, on a national scale, in the nineteenth century. Of the fourfold poverty (see above), the agrarian poverty, and the first-phase of industrialization poverty have been replaced by the population-explosion poverty of developing countries and their increasing contrast with industrialized countries.

e. The communist revolution has succeeded in some non-western countries and is expanding to other countries of Asia, Africa, and Latin America.

For the Christian church, in comparison with the nineteenth-century situation, the problem has become proportionately aggravated:

a. The partial success of Christian diaconate and social welfare action in attacking the national poverty problem in western Christian countries stands in sharp contrast to the traditional helplessness and sterility of Christian thinking and action facing the war problem.

b. There is a real danger that the present-day Christian diaconate on a worldwide scale (Inter-Church Aid; Church World Service, etc.) may repeat the tragic errors of the Christian diaconate in western Europe in the middle of the nineteenth century—an error which can be summed up as a micro-approach to a macro-structural problem. The error does not consist in the micro-approach itself, which has great merits and is of the utmost urgency, but in the inability and partial blindness in facing the macro-structural problem of a failing world economy.

c. In spite of the growth of an ecumenical community of Christian thinking and action on a worldwide scale, this community has not even a shadow of the coherence and consistency which national churches had and still dispose of. Moreover, the overwhelming majority of Christians is living in the western, affluent countries and the demographic trend of world population growth will even tip the balance more and more to that side. Western Christian countries are increasingly becoming the world's "Christian bourgeoisie."

d. The Christian church is just in the beginning of rethinking her traditional approach to social problems, and she has hardly begun to discover the dimensions and the unprecedented character of worldwide poverty in our century.

e. The church's failure to give an adequate answer to the ideology of class struggle in the nineteenth century, has made her enter the second half of the twentieth century utterly unprepared for the challenge of communism on a worldwide scale. The church has succeeded, throughout church history, in adapting herself to successive social changes, but she stands puzzled and confused facing the unprecedented consequences of the industrializing process for the structure of international relations.

MISSIONS AND SERVICE

There exists, to be sure, a certain tension between "evangelization" and "service," between "word" and "deed," between "kerygma" and "diaconia." This tension does not coincide with the tension between the tradition of foreign missions and the recently developed programs of inter-church aid, but there is, nevertheless, some relationship between both questions. The integration between the International Missionary Council and the World Council of Churches and, recently in the United States, the unification of Foreign Missions and Church World Service into the integrated Division of Overseas Ministries have already meant important steps toward overcoming a theological distinction and a tension between different traditions and approaches which we cannot allow to lead to wrong contrasts and to inadequate working methods. Evangelism and service, mission and aid, are essentially two aspects of one and the same Gospel.

Our gratitude for the progress, resulting from this fundamental and practical integration should not, however, blind us to some implicit questions.

In the middle of the nineteenth century, Wichern's program of the "Innere Mission" was by itself borne of the vision of a unity between word and deed. Because he failed, however, in a radical diagnosis and consequent therapy of the socio-political macro-structural situation, his diaconal action remained a series of emergency rescue actions and his preaching more and more developed into a pietistic consolation message. The lesson to be learned from this experience is that our present-day integration between foreign missions and service overseas is no guarantee that the trend will not go in an analogous direction this time on a worldwide scale.

There exists a certain connection between:

a. foreign missions
b. inter-church aid
c. western macro-assistance.

Since western macro-assistance is, on the one hand, involved in the dilemma of the conflict between developed and underdeveloped countries and, on the other hand, is unavoidably connected with the cold war strategy of western countries, any form of ecumenical inter-church aid and, *a fortiori,* any kind of overseas service of western churches are predestined to get involved in this dilemma. Integration between missions and service will mean that the work of missions will get definitely entangled in this dilemma. And, conversely, the missionary witness faces more seriously and more inescapably than ever before the crucial test as to whether or not it includes a prophetic message about the overarching dilemma of macro-structural international relations and of a socio-economic world order.

The experience of the Division of Inter-Church Aid, Refugee and World Service of the World Council of Churches, has already led to the insight that the basic questions which the missionary movement has been facing during its long tradition cannot be escaped by any kind of aid which pretends to be more than a series of emergency acts in case of civil war, epidemics, or catastrophes. Missions have been summoning foreign peoples, living in age-old cultural patterns, to conversion. Inter-Church Aid has the strategic function wherein it transmits to missions the insight that effective aid has to come to grips with the macro-structural dimensions of the socio-economic order, and wherein it transfers to the whole field of assistance to underdeveloped countries the fundamental conviction of missions that long-term aid implies a basic transformation of the traditional pattern of civilization. It is here that prophetic witness and the crucial question of the "takeoff" on the road to technocratic development are intermingled, meeting each other within the ellipse of our main theme "prophecy in a technocratic era."

BREAKING THROUGH
THE VICIOUS CIRCLES

The basic dilemma of the development issue can be characterized in the question, how to break through two vicious circles:

    a. the vicious circle of underdevelopment;

    b. the vicious circle of development.

The vicious circle of underdevelopment consists of the self-perpetuating character of the traditional "neolithic" civilization, rooted in age-old religions. The vicious circle of development consists in the concatenation of competition, cold war, and armament. Both circles are intersecting and mutually aggravating each other's problems. The total complex of these intertwined lines is the basic dilemma of the total process of development, seen in a planetary view. The fundamental challenge to the Christian mission in our century is the question of where and how to break through the vicious circles, each by itself and together as an interdependent whole.

RETHINKING OUR MISSION

Looking in a bird's-eye view at the questions we have been discussing or have been hinting at, it may have become obvious that the dimensions of the Christian mission in our time are wider and its implications more complicated than our traditional view has allowed us to guess. The strategic issues can be summed up as follows.

a. Our mission is involved in the ongoing line of Christian history. It has a "here" (in our case, the United States) and a "now" (the technocratic era), which both have their relationship to the "here" (Jerusalem) and the "now" (Anno Domini) of the Incarnation.

b. This relationship implies the necessity and the possibility of "prophecy in a technocratic era," actualizing the message of the Old and New Testament for our time.

c. The crucial question regarding the role of the laity is whether or not it has an adequate answer to the challenge of a "world come of age."

d. The encounter with the worldwide challenge of communism compels us to a comprehensive rethinking of our missionary task.

e. Christian service in the non-western world is involved in all dilemmas of the development issue.

f. The test case for our witness is whether we shall be able to break through the vicious circles of a world in process of development.

What are the consequences of these points? For each issue, the following suggestions are to be considered:

a. Mission begins at the "home base." Bringing the Gospel "overseas" can never be an alibi for escaping the radical questions at home; otherwise the missionary movement degenerates into colonialist romanticism.

b. We should devote much more serious attention to the prophetic message of the Old Testament, being a comprehensive approach to the total structures of society.

c. The missionary movement has to pass the dividing line between the era of mobilizing the lay forces for the evangelization of the world and the present-day issue of a radical confrontation of a secular world with our message.

d. From traditional thinking in terms of mission fields, we have to pass into concepts of confrontation, dialogue, preparedness to hear and absorb profound criticism and devastating questions. The best service may be the "spiritual diaconate" of bearing together with our fellowmen our common and our mutual unsolved problems. This refers in particular to our attitude to communism: it has deprived us of our "mission fields," but we owe to it the immense service of a total and radical criticism of our whole Christian and missionary tradition.

e. We should find ways to put our micro-structural aid and service to countries overseas within the context of the great macro-structural problems of international relations and of a socio-economic world order.

f. All talk about the problems and frustrations of non-western countries which does not realize that the problems and frustrations of our own developed countries are even more serious and are aggravating the problems of the non-western world is onesided and therefore deceitful. Only a comprehensive dealing with the total world situation is adequate to our present-day missionary consciousness.

It will be a long way to realizing this rethinking of our missionary task. What we most urgently need, therefore, is an independent center for basic, comprehensive research and for preparing long-term policy. This center should consist of an interdisciplinary team that is free from divisions between existing organizations and is free for laying links with and bringing together any organization, group, or individuals which it needs for its work and is free to organize in any form which it considers necessary and adequate. This center, to be sure, will not be in a position to make policy, for this will be incumbent upon those bodies which bear direct responsibility for action, but it has to function as a means of preparing, over a long term, new policies and it has to open up new dimensions of thinking.

Its functions can, in broad outline, be sketched as follows:

1. It is, to some extent, comparable to the "research laboratory" of a big factory. Industrial production is unthinkable without research, which is continuously concerned with technological progress and new inventions. This industrial research has a medium position between the university and the factory.

Analogously, the center should be definitely better equipped than and be built up differently from the familiar ecumenical and missionary study departments, though it should have in common with them a close connection with practice and action and a ready availability. Having, on the other hand, close affinity to the university structure, it should definitely break through the familiar discipline divisions and specializations and be focused upon arranging unprecedented interdisciplinary teamwork.

2. It has to carry out basic research, which means research which is not concerned with analysis of surface phenomena and accidental situations, but with fundamental presupposition and background trends. This basic research will, above all, be distinguished by two special concerns:

    a. confrontation of fundamental analysis of biblical prophecy with fundamental analysis of modern technocracy.

    b. definite concern with future trends and developments. In other words, its research will bear a "futurological" character.

3. Its research should be focused upon comprehensive thinking and be primarily concerned with promoting cross-fertilization, cutting breaches in specialization walls, building bridges across traditional cleavages between disciplines, breaking down psychological barriers and preoccupations between different faculties and scientific modes of thinking. This interdisciplinary teamwork should be conducted around a concrete long-term research project. The function of this project should not consist of specialized contributions but in making unprecedented combinations and interconnections between specializations. Thereby it can have a thought-provoking, inspiring influence in many directions.

4. The style of work should also be comprehensive, in that it is concerned with the fundamental unity of traditionally divided and contradictory dimensions. It should be:

a. thinking about today from the viewpoint of tomorrow, instead of dealing with today and tomorrow as a continuation of yesterday;

b. recognizing the basic identity of logos and ethos;

c. giving priority to the macro-structural approach and recognizing the basic unity of the macro-structural and the micro-structural dimension;

d. denying an essential contrast between theory and practice and recognizing the far-reaching, future-determining significance of theories.

5. The center should have an outspoken lay character. It has to break radically through the separation between theology and exact science. It has to develop a method whereby the familiar theological approach is irresistibly drawn into the orbit of the exact sciences and whereby, on the other hand, the exact sciences are challenged to give fundamental answers which bear an implicit theological character. The teamwork within the center should be done without any reference to one's traditional labels and should not take account of any contrast between institutional church and world.

6. The center could start with a long-term study project focusing upon the subject of development. A fundamental theme could be "development of the world in this generation." This theme could be approached from the viewpoint, "prophecy in a technocratic era." The center could be developed in keeping with the development of this project. After a series of hearings a selected team should design and start the project, beginning with an experimental period of one year. A grant from special funds may be needed to start the project.

INDEX